ROGER MADE ME DO IT

By
Ed Zukusky

Dedication

To Roger, who made me do it. I am forever thankful that you did. To Nancy, thank you for fighting the good fight in helping me edit this book. But mostly, thank you for encouraging me to finish this book. It is very much appreciated. To Leann, thank you for slapping me alongside the head, when I needed it, to keep me on the straight and narrow. To Dianne, thank you for supporting me through all of this. I think it was more of an ordeal for you than it was for me. Or maybe a tie!!! To all of you in the classic car community that I may have abused, nothing personal, it was really all in fun… Well! At least most of it was ☺…

TABLE OF CONTENTS

Introduction	The Author and the Book	4
Chapter 1	How Did I Get Here?	7
Chapter 2	Roger Made Me Do It	15
Chapter 3	My Marauder	23
Chapter 4	Backcountry Road Trip	39
Chapter 5	Last Train to Twitsville	55
Chapter 6	Local Car Shows	67
Chapter 7	Curse of the Beast	85
Chapter 8	Broncos and Pit Bulls	101
Chapter 9	Hilton Head Concours d' Elegance	111
Chapter 10	Boca Raton Concours d' Elegance	121
Chapter 11	Welcome to White, Georgia	131
Epilogue		143
Addendum	A collection of "Stuff"	145

Introduction
The Author and the Book

To understand the crazy world of classic cars, you need a guide, someone who's been there, someone who knows their way around, someone who's made a few mistakes, learned from them, and can show you how to be successful in this crazy world. **Well ... That's not me.**

If, on the other hand, you just want to take a ride through this crazy world with someone who has made all of the possible mistakes known to mankind and continues to make new ones, *then I'm your guy...*

I grew up in the '50s drag racing flathead Fords on back roads. The '60s was the Muscle Car era. I was deep into it with a 409 Chevy, a 440 Charger and more. Then came marriage, a family and SUVs. My love affair with cars was left to admiration from a distance.

    Then in the early 2000s I got re-acquainted with a good friend, Roger Papp, who turned me on to restoring, owning and showing classic cars. He took me out of a boring retirement and back to an era when cars had character and performance was king. I owe him a great debt for that. This book chronicles my journey through this crazy world. It highlights individual events and revelations that shaped, or miss-shaped, my life as I stumbled and fumbled my way through this world. It is mostly a true story filled in with much exaggeration and satire. I hope you enjoy it.

Ed Zukusky

--- *READER ALERT* ---

The first chapter of this book has little to do with classic cars. I know the book is about my life with classic cars, *but,* I had a life (most recently retirement) before classic cars. This chapter has everything to do with why I became involved in classic cars. Like everything else in the book it is based on real events in my life. These real events are punctuated with fiction, heavily laced with exaggeration and loosely wrapped with satire. If, in reading this book, you are able to discern what's fact, what's fiction and what's exaggeration or satire then you are way ahead of me. Please keep it to yourself. At this point, I really don't want to know...

Chapter 1
How Did I Get Here?
Retirement Crisis and the Checkout Lady.

I was doomed from the start. It's a gruesome story, but this is how I became a classic car guy. My father was a backyard mechanic who raced four banger Fords at the local dirt track on the weekends. Four banger Fords were four cylinder Ford engines that were *souped-up* and put in stripped down Ford Model A chassis. They weren't much on the straight-a-ways, which weren't very long anyway, but they were hell coming out of the corners. I never saw my Dad race but the stories were always there, and I guess this background was a part of my genetic makeup. Couple this with my teenage years being the '50s era of customized hotrods, and you can see why I love cars. I've been into the *car thing* for as long as I can remember. The '50s and '60s were my *car thing* years. The '70s through the '90s were marriage, family, Little League games, etc., with the *car thing* sort of fading into the background.

When I retired in 2001, after an outstanding two year career of being unemployed, my son was just starting college. Financially, the college years put some stress on our budget. Thanks to some savings, and to my wife Dianne and her steady job, we survived. With the financial stress of the college years, my retirement ended up not being the *Golden Years* of free spending on vacations, travel and worldly goods that I had anticipated. It was a bummer and a disappointment that I had trouble dealing with. As these retirement years went on, I slowly became a victim of *Retirement Crisis*, which is much like a *Mid-life Crisis*, but without the mid-life funds to buy a Porsche and go nuts. In between watching *Star Trek* reruns and Jay Leno, I puttered and potted; mowed and trimmed; and slowly sank into the depression phase of *Retirement Crisis*. I was surly, non-talkative and rude, and extremely good at it.

My time of enlightenment started in the checkout line at the local Foodbuy Supermarket. Normally when I go through Foodbuy's checkout line there is a cashier about 16 years old that always asks me, smiling cheerfully, "How are you doing today?" I know this is Foodbuy policy, and I know she doesn't really give a damn how I am today, so being my surly self I am noncommittal, or mumble something like, "I don't know" or, "You don't want to know." As these responses are not in the Foodbuy Policy Manual, and are contrary to the 16 year old's world of *everything is wonderful*, the young cashier becomes numb and quiet. Mission accomplished! The baggers, who are at least 20 years older than I am, understand completely and waves of pity wash down the checkout lane toward me. *Let me out of here!*

I began to dread Foodbuy and these checkout encounters. Then one day in the Foodbuy checkout line, I notice that the cashier is not a 16 year old but a mature good looking woman in her late '30s. She is still doing the Foodbuy policy of "How are you doing today?" but maintaining a conversation with each customer, and she appears to be interested in each one. Suddenly fear sets in. I can't be my surly self and do my usual act of, *"You don't want to know"* as this cashier appears to be a nice person that seems to actually care about people. I can't be my normal surly self to her, *can I?*

Uh Oh!

Then I remember my friend Jack, a very outgoing, happy guy, whose response to "How are you doing today?" many times was, "If I was doing any better I'd be you." This almost always got a smile and started a conversation. *Can I do this?* I begin repeating to myself "If I was doing any better I'd be you" over and over. "If I was doing any better I'd be you"... The line continues to move and the cashier continues to be nice to everyone. When my turn finally comes sweat is pouring off me, and the nice cashier looks up at me, smiles and says "How are you doing today?" Fear grabs me, my mouth goes dry, and I panic and blurt out:

"If I was doing any better I'd be doing you."

Uh Oh!!!

Time stands still. The checkout line freezes. Silence roars through Foodbuy. For what seems like hours, we are frozen in time. Then the nice cashier looks up from her scanning, smiles at me and says, "Honey, you ain't ever going to be doing that good." Foodbuy exhales, baggers giggle, scanner sounds take over the silence, I empty my wallet and run to the car.

Back to Foodbuy…
Because of my traumatic experience at Foodbuy I have been shopping at Shopnstuff for the last 2 weeks. I have wandered their aisles like a rat in a maze, never finding exactly what I want. Nothing is where it should be, so I am buying and eating products I have never heard of. Nothing seems right, nothing tastes the same. Also, I am absolutely positive that all of the 16 year old checkers from Foodbuy are now working, and smiling, at Shopnstuff. It's a conspiracy.

I feast tonight…

My life is in chaos. I am left with no choice. I am going back to Foodbuy.

I'm back in Foodbuy; I can find everything I need. Life is good. I have Spam, peanut butter and Italian bread in my cart. *I feast tonight!*

But I know I have to check out eventually. I survey the checkout lines and spot the *doing you* checkout lady. Thinking quickly, I immediately go over to the only other open line… just as it closes. "Sorry we're closed, please use the other line" smiles the 16 year old checker. I stand still, frozen. The 16 year old checker smiles again and repeats "Sorry we're closed, please use the other line." I beg and yell out, "I have only three items in my cart!" The 16 year old checker smiles, chews down hard on her gum and says "I'm outta here" and she's gone. I am now in panic mode! Do I sneak out of the store and leave my food behind or do I go through the *doing you* checkout lady's line? I am just minutes away from a Spam and peanut butter sandwich--I can't abort now--I can't, I need my Spam--I'm going for it!!!

I'm now in the *doing you* checkout lady's lane. As I move toward the front of the line I begin to sweat and realize that I can't go through with this. I need out of here! As I go to back up out of the checkout line I find that a rather large woman has blocked the lane, and my escape, with a cart piled high with Oreos and ice cream. I am trapped. As I wait my turn, I try to think of ways to disguise myself. Maybe no eye contact, or maybe a smile and a little higher voice, or maybe just bluff my way through like nothing ever happened. I turn my cap backwards, put on my sun glasses and wait my turn...

Okay! It's now my turn. The nice checkout lady starts to say "How are you doing..." and recognizes me. "Haven't seen you in a while," she says with a smile. It's panic time again!!! Sweat pours off me, but her smile relaxes me. Maybe if I apologize to this nice checkout lady everything will be OK. I collect myself, take a deep breath, smile, and calmly say:

"I am really sorry about last time. There is no way I would even *think* about doing you."

Uh Oh!

Foodbuy goes silent, scanners stop beeping, baggers cover their eyes and the nice checkout lady stares at me for what seems to be hours. Then the fat lady behind me begins beating on me with a bag of Oreos. Cheers go up throughout

Foodbuy, baggers drop to their knees, Oreos are flying everywhere. As the Oreo-induced pain starts to take over my brain the nice checkout lady smiles at me. I smile back (hopefully), and then she passes the fat lady one of those bar type things that they use to separate each customers groceries. As the fat lady winds up with the bar thing, I bolt for the door.

As a 'Weapon'?

Spam & Peanut Butter...

I don't know how they found me. Maybe they traced a credit card? Maybe they posted my photo at the door and someone recognized me? That might be it, because my photo *is* posted at the door. At least the letter said it was. I received a registered letter from Foodbuy stating that I was banned from their store for life. Should I attempt to enter the store they would file charges of sexual harassment. Sexual harassment! There was no sexual harassment. It was pure *Verbal Senility*, a common side effect of *Retirement Crisis*.

I AM NOT A BAD PERSON, I JUST ACT LIKE ONE!!!

I feel myself entering into Spam and Peanut Butter sandwich withdrawal as I try to understand what is happening. I have been unable to get my Spam fix, as Shopnstuff doesn't carry Spam. I ask the store manager why. I am told it's a religious thing. Huh? What religion? I demand. The store manager says "The Church of Good Taste," and he immediately starts cracking up, assistant managers start snickering and 16 year old checkers begin giggling. I quickly jump into *verbal senility* mode and yell out, "Everyone likes a smartass." *Take that!* I turn to leave and bump into a large display of ammonia bottles. The bottles teeter back and forth. As I watch, in what seems to be slow motion, bottles of ammonia go crashing to the floor. Ammonia vapors quickly engulf the store, Store Managers scream out, baggers run for the restrooms, and the 16 year old checkers continue to smile while sniffing the air. With eyes burning, I bolt for the door.

So, having successfully eliminated Foodbuy and Shopnstuff as contenders for my food dollars, I move on. With my cap on backwards, sunglasses, and my beard now dyed red, I cautiously feast on hot dogs and Big Slurps at my corner Pickfast while planning my next move… **Next move!!!** *What next move? I don't have a next move!!!* My life is down to Big Slurps and hot dogs!!! Suddenly a massive dose of *Logic*, from some deep recess in my brain, screams at me. "**Get a Life!**" Huh? I've got a life--but--but--it's boring. A 1,000 watt light bulb suddenly goes off in my head and I can see! I know! I know! *I need a hobby!*

NOTE: A hobby is the anti-job. In a job you do as little work as possible and you get money in. In a hobby you bust your butt working hard as you pay money out.

OK, I need a hobby, but what? Are Golf & Fishing hobbies? Nah, they're just sports you do occasionally, not something to keep me busy and get me out of *retirement crisis* mode. I guess collecting things can be a hobby. I've done that before. I wasn't very good at it, as far as it being a hobby. Actually I was very good at the collecting part, which my wife said was the problem. Like when I decided to collect HO Trains. I was able to collect 184 different trains in less than 2 weeks. Not the right way, I'm told, and I was on a roll too. I could have cornered the market by the end of the year. Sure there were storage issues and financial issues, but you can rent warehouses and it's an investment…

And then I talked to Roger...

Chapter 2
Roger Made Me Do It!!!

*An old friend wants **me** to restore a car!!!*
He knows not what he does...

Roger Papp and I were best of friends when we worked together back in the early '80s. I had lost track of Roger, but one day as I was browsing the internet I came across Roger's name as the President of the South Georgia AACA (whatever the hell that is). The short story is that I contacted Roger and he and his wife Leann came down to Florida to visit us. I asked Roger what he has been doing since he retired, and he pulls out a massive book full of pictures of classic cars that he had restored. Awesome!!! Great cars! It brings back memories, and I ask a lot of questions. Awesome!!!

Roger suggests that *"I"* should consider restoring a classic car. *"No, can't…"* Roger says he will help me. *"No, can't…"* He will be my mentor and teach me. *"No, can't…"* Roger begins to give up on me but then continues on, explaining to me why he enjoys the *classic car hobby.*

Whoa! What did he say? Did he say *hobby*? Yes! He said *hobby*!!!

I'm looking for one of those. Could this be it, my new hobby? It is! It will be! I'm hooked! I'm excited!

I tell Roger that I want to start by getting one of the cars I used to own back in the day. I'm on a roll; I love this. First I'll get the 63 Impala SS 409 I had, then I'll get the 69 Charger R/T 440 I had and then…

What's that Roger? $60,000 for the Impala and $75,000 for the Charger.

$60,000 Impala!!!!!!

I quickly fall back into depression mode. Roger begins to talk me out of my depression by explaining that there are a lot of neat cars out there that are not expensive. I just need to decide what kind of car I want and we will find one that is not expensive.

No problem! I know exactly what kind of car I want! I want a muscle car, big block, bucket seats, floor shift, and faster than Spam through a large intestine.

$75,000 Charger R/T!!!!!!

That's what I want, something really cool, *but not expensive.*

What's that Roger? Have I ever considered HO Trains as a hobby?

Oh, you're kidding… Right? You are kidding?

So Roger and I have agreed that we will restore a classic car together. One problem: How do I explain this new, and probably expensive, hobby to my wife? I suppose I could just tell her that I am going to do it. Nah! I need to rationalize it, make it sound like this is something that will rejuvenate my life, improve my health and make me a better human being. I begin developing various scenarios as I try to predict my wife's response. I laboriously memorize various justifications based on the responses I'm anticipating from my wife. Finally, I have all of the bases covered. I'm prepared:

With great confidence I calmly say, "Dear, you know how I feel that a hobby is something I need. Well I want to restore a classic car and Roger will help me."

My wife looks at me and says "Huh?"

Unprepared for this specific response I blurt out, "Roger is making me restore a classic car with him. He says it will be good for me and that our friendship depends on it."

Uh Oh!

My wife screams out, "You son of a ..."

Actually, that's what I anticipated she would say. What she actually said was, "If that's what you want."

Does anyone know what that actually means? Does it mean "OK, have fun dear," or "OK, but I'll never speak to you again," or "OK, but I will kill you in your sleep"?

I call Roger and tell him we are a go. He asks: "How did your wife take it?" I begin to say fine, not a problem, but I can't lie to Roger. Roger is one of the true good guys. He will do anything for you. There is no better friend. So I tell Roger, sort of, about the conversation. He sounds visibly shaken. Roger knows that my wife's family is from New Jersey and that she has a cousin named Guido. I try to calm Roger down, but I know, as soon as I hang up, Roger will be on the phone with ADT getting his security system updated.

Cousin Guido

In any case, I have no control over the outcome, so a somewhat paranoid Roger and I are off to search the wilds of the internet for my classic muscle car.

I have a hobby; is that cool or what?

The Search Begins...

So off I went with Roger, my consultant, leading me. I spent my time searching the internet, going to car shows and looking at newspaper ads. Roger did the same and because he lives in White, Georgia, and I live in Bradenton, Florida, 500 miles apart, we communicated mostly via email sending pictures and information on cars back and forth. This went on for months. I was pretty hesitant and indecisive and very good at both. Roger finally said, "You have to decide what you want in a car and then we need to go look for *that car*." I said I wanted a muscle car but I can't find one. He said, "I know that! What are the *specifics* you want?"

I said, "I *specifically* want a muscle car." *Well, that was the wrong answer.* Now, most people have a range of emotions: calm, irritated, upset, mad, etc., and slowly move from one to the other. But Roger is different.

Roger is the ultimate calm, logical, nice guy without any great range of emotions beyond calm. 99.9 % of the time Roger is calm and logical, doesn't get mad, rolls with the punches, etc. But 0.1% of the time Roger leaves this calm state, bypasses all other emotions, and flash forwards to *totally teed off*. Well, my answer put Roger in flash forward mode and just before he was about to go *nova*, I was able to "sorry about that" him back into calm.

So we started over with Roger asking the questions.

How much do you want to spend? What type of car? What features do you want? Etc. Etc. Etc. Well, he had me backed in a corner. So I came up with my parameters:
1. It had to be different, no 1955 - 57 Chevys or Mustangs; *everybody has one.*
2. It had to be a muscle car that was in my price range. The 427 Ford, the Impala SSs, the Charger R/Ts, etc., were not even close to my price range.

OK, Roger said, "What is your definition of a muscle car?" I thought about the ones I had owned back-in-the-day and decided:
1. At least 400+ cubic inches, bucket seats, console and a floor shift.
2. Because I live in Florida, I needed A/C. Preferably on the car, but aftermarket would do. But that also had to fit within my budget.

So, tallyho! The hunt was on. First on the hit parade were 1966-67 Dodge Chargers; cool cars. I couldn't afford the Hemi powered ones, but the 440s were reasonably priced, not rare, but not common either. I almost bought one but chickened out at the last minute.

Big Green Car...

Next, I came across this big green car. I didn't recognize it as something I'd seen back-in-the-day. The write up on it said it was a 1969 Mercury Marauder X-100. It had a big block 429 with 360 HP, bucket seats, and a console with floor shift (a horseshoe shaped floor shift...) *COOL!!!* It was everything I was looking for and it was priced within my budget; up near the top, but still within. The only problem was I hated the color. Green and I do not get along. It might be that St. Patty's day *green beer* back when I was 18 or it might be the fact that anything green that grows in Florida, grass, weeds, trees, etc., makes me break out in a rash if I get within 10 feet of it.

I could paint the car, which would blow my budget big time, or I could look for another Marauder X-100. So I looked for another Marauder X-100. As I learned more about them I became *Marauder hooked*. Roger and I trucked on and quickly found out that X-100s were few and far between. As time rolled on Roger tried a few times to point me in another direction but I was determined. I was also stubborn and pigheaded, which I can be very good at.

The first X-100 we found was a beautiful dark blue car. I was ready to buy it, checkbook in hand, when Roger lassoed me and held me down. Logic and experience spewed forth from Roger. What if the car isn't exactly what the owner says it is? What if the pictures don't show some problem areas? Etc. Etc. Etc. I said, "Roger, he's a classic car guy he wouldn't do that, would he?" I don't remember the rest of our conversation too well except something about being *a dumb a$$* and that *we are going to check out the car*!

I explained to Roger that the car was in Idaho and I didn't think we could get there from here. Roger then explained to me that there was a national company that had qualified inspectors who would check out the car for us. Roger worked for the company on occasion and thought he could get us a discount rate. So we hired an inspector and awaited his qualified report on the car. It came back quickly and was very direct. It said we didn't want this car. The inspector also said he was unable to complete the inspection or take any pictures, as the cloud of blue smoke that engulfed the car, once it was started appeared to be toxic and he was unable to get to (find) the car to shut it off.

The second car we found was black and beautiful. Lots of pictures, black on black with a black leather interior. I loved it. I believe black is the only color for a car, especially a big car. If I would have bought that green X-100 I would have painted it black. Having found a black X-100, I'm in heaven and begin looking for the check book when this little voice in the back of my brain shouts, "We *are* going to check out the car!" *Where have I heard that before?*

So we hire another qualified inspector and send him out to check on the black beauty. A week later we get a report in the mail from the inspector. It contained 15 pages of notes and lots of pictures. The first picture in the report jumps out at me. The car pictured in the ad had Kelsey Hayes aluminum wheels on it. This car is up on cinder blocks in a garage. The next picture is of 2 cases of empty Rust-Oleum black spray paint cans in the back of the garage. I note that the inspector's report is not very positive on the car's paint job especially the *painted* leather seats. The car in the pictures looks like it went through 20 years of being *rode hard and put away wet.*

Uh-oh. Could these be 20 year old pictures? Now that I think of it, the one picture in the ad of the owner with his car did look strange. In the picture the owner had on a powder blue leisure suit. If it wasn't for the fact that the car was in Alabama, I might have considered that strange.

Well, that's two strikes and $700 worth of inspectors, but I'm hardheaded and ready to go off again looking for my Marauder. Roger is tired and is bouncing back and forth trying to get me to do something. "How about a Chevy? How about a Mustang? Have you considered HO trains?" all fall on deaf ears

We continue to search, while I put ads on Mercury and Marauder web sites saying, "Please sell me an X-100, please, pretty please…"

Chapter 3
My Marauder
Buying and restoring a classic car, with very little help from me.

A few weeks later I get an email saying, "I saw your ad, are you still looking for a Marauder?"

I answer back that I am and ask for pictures and information. The pictures come back, and the car is black and beautiful. I quickly scan all of the pictures looking for guys in leisure suits. I don't see any leisure suits, although one person does look a little strange. But it is Ohio…

The guy explains that he bought the Marauder from a friend that needed the money. His friend had the car for a few years and never had the time or money to finish it. The guy re-chromed the rear bumper and fixed a few things and now it was up for sale. He explained that he was just trying to get back the money he had in the car.

Roger asked, "What has to be done to the car to make it a show car?"

The guy responded with, "It's not a Concours car but if you buff out the paint it will be ready to show." We exchange a number of telephone calls and emails back and forth and both Roger and I like the guy. He seems to be a good guy but... (WHOA!) I don't hear any buts. Where is that little voice in the back of my mind that shouts "we *are* going to check out the car?" And why is Roger saying nothing about checking out this car? Me, I'm thinking that I don't want to spend another $350 for an inspector, and my guess is that Roger is thinking *Just buy a damn car...PLEASE!*

Well, Roger and I agree. I will buy the car. We have a deal. I am now a Marauder X-100 owner and all I have to do now is *buff out the paint and go show the car.* We make arrangements to get the car shipped to Roger's house in Georgia so that we, actually Roger, can check it out for any small problems before we *buff out the paint and go show the car.*

A week and a half later Roger gets a call from a car transport company informing us that my car will be delivered in three days. Roger gives the driver the directions to the Wal-Mart store in Cartersville, Georgia. White, Georgia, is the ultimate small town, not even a traffic light, and there isn't any place that a tractor trailer could actually park and unload a car. Cartersville is the next town over from White and is only 10 miles from Roger's house so it's no big deal. Roger will make the pickup there and drive the car back.

The big day arrives. Roger calls me and says that the driver is just pulling into Wal-Mart and Roger is on his way there. Roger promises to call me as soon as he gets the car back to his house. Visions of buffing dance through my head, *Buff out the paint and go show the car.* I am psyched!!!

It's been three hours and no call from Roger. What's

going on? Maybe he stopped to buy a buffer and some wax? Yeah, that must be it. Then the phone rings. It's Roger. I scream into the phone, "Roger, did you get the car?"

In his normal calm voice Roger says "Yes it's at the house." Then silence.

"So tell me about it!" I shout anxiously.

Roger begins, "The good news is that it will run 90 mph with no problem."

The bad news is:
- The left rear quarter, which we did not get a picture of, is in primer.
- The paint is beyond the help of any buffer Roger ever heard of.
- The engine compartment looks like raccoons have been living it.
- The raccoons were smart to live in the engine compartment because the interior is filthy.
- And, best of all, the car transport driver scraped the side of the car backing it off the trailer and also destroyed the wheel well chrome.

I scream out, "Will buffing fix that?" No answer. In a state of shock, I say to Roger, "Tell me something good about the car." Silence lasts for days… (Seems like it).

Then Roger, with his normal calm voice slowly edging toward flash forward mode, says, "It's big! It's Black! It's…. It's… It's a damn Black **Widow**!"

My mind reels and I blurt out, *"The only **Widow** in this will be my wife, after she shoots me for buying this piece of junk."*

JUST DELIVERED
OOPS! Not so nice car

Reality hits. Buffing is now just a distant memory. I know my Marauder X-100 is not perfect, and I know it needs some work, but Roger and I will work on it. It will be good.

Also on the good side, this was a christening of sorts, as from this day forward my Marauder would always be known as the **Widow**.

First Look...
Two days later, having put everything at home on hold for 2 weeks, I am anxious and apprehensive as I fly up to Roger's house in Georgia to see my Marauder for the first time. Roger has been very kind lately, telling me what a good car it seems to be. If it was anyone but Roger I would question the kind words. Still, Roger's version of a good car and how I am going to feel when I see it might be a bit different. I'm worried that I will be disappointed and slip back into *retirement crisis* mode.

Roger meets me at the Atlanta airport and we leave in Roger's truck for a one hour drive to White, Georgia. Roger starts going over what has to be done to the car. Because the car is going to be more of a driver car than a show car, Roger's emphasis is on getting it road ready. He goes through his list: A/C doesn't work; engine needs to be checked out and tuned (sparkplugs, points, etc.); all of the fluids need to be changed; the transmission need to be checked out thoroughly; exhaust system needs work; etc. My mind reels, *what happened to "buff and show"?* What have I got myself into?

We finally arrive at Roger's house and I'm nervous. We go into Roger's garage and there it sits: my Marauder. Roger was right. It's big. It's black. It's a damn Black Widow! It's also like Roger said: dirty, in primer, and scraped-up. But ... **It's BEAUTIFUL!! I LOVE IT!!** I ask Roger if I can drive it. He says, "It's your car, the keys are in it."

I start it and it sounds powerful. As I back it out of the garage I suddenly realize how big and heavy it is just turning it around in the driveway. My mind races around in circles. A 429 engine with 360 horsepower will be lucky to get this big animal even moving. 90 miles an hour, sure! But how many hours will it take to get to that speed? Zero to sixty in less than half a day? **What the hell did I buy???** Roger explains that the car has 580 lb. ft. of torque at just 2,800 RPM so it should accelerate quickly. *"Yeah right!!!"* I murmur under my breath, not wanting Roger to hear. I carefully get out to the highway, which is a winding back road and the car purrs along. Well at least it can cruise along with little effort.

Roger suddenly says, "This is a straight away, stomp on it." So I do and **"Whoa!!!"** the big beast lurches forward. The speedometer needle sweeps across the dial like a windshield wiper in high speed. The speedometer winds higher. 360 horses scream, while gulping down huge quantities of air and gas as the big animal continues to accelerate, and "*I become one with it…*"

Whoa!! Wait a minute… That's Roger yelling… Suddenly my *oneness* is shattered by Roger's screams of "slow down there are curves ahead," and I slow down--sort of--reluctantly…

We follow the curving road to its dead end at a deserted (late November in Georgia) boat launching ramp at Allatoona Lake. I turn the Widow around and realize we are in a long flat parking area by the boat launch ramp that goes for about an eighth of a mile before it gets to the winding road. I stop, look over at Roger, and with a big grin I stomp the gas to the floor!!! The tires scream and smoke as the Widow fights to get traction and starts its one eighth mile journey toward the winding road. The engine roars as the car accelerates, the transmission shifts hard out of first gear and the Widow lurches forward. *My oneness is back*, and then I hear Roger calmly say, "We need to take it easy until everything is checked out." My mind screams out "**I don't think so,**" Roger repeats, "we need to take it easy until everything is checked out." My mind screams out again **"I don't think so!!!"**... But, from that recess deep in the back of my mind, "**Logic**" lashes out and whacks me in the back of the head. "**Logic**" screams down at me and floods my brain with reason, and I am forced to agree with Roger. So I back off, reluctantly, and we head back to Roger's house. I *may need to change my underwear...*

I'm in love...   Let the restoration begin!!!

Road Ready...

The next 2 weeks consisted of going from shop to shop. Transmissions, engine, A/C, exhaust, etc. are all addressed. All goes well, with the car checking out as probably a true 50,000 mile car that has never had the engine out of it, or the heads off of it. Roger guessed that the A/C might be a big ticket item, $1,500 or so to rebuild it. Roger's A/C mechanic put in a new expansion valve, charged me $150, and we had cold air. The exhaust leak was found to be in the exhaust manifold, which would also be a big ticket item if we could find an exhaust manifold for a 1969 429 engine. Roger's exhaust guy sends us over to a welding shop he knows and 15 minutes and $50 later the exhaust leak is history. Back to the exhaust guy, who installs a set of deep throaty Flowmaster mufflers and the Widow is now sounding like she could chew up and spit out the Batmobile for breakfast.

I could be out of underwear real soon.

Our next project was the interior, which was filthy. The carpet looked like wild boars had rooted through it looking for food. The new carpet we ordered came in and we started to take the seats out of the car. One problem that I had with the car is that the seat was not adjustable height-wise. I'm 6'2' and 5 foot of me is from the waist up, so my head was close to touching the roof of the car during normal driving. In taking the seats out we found 2 inch high wooden blocks, painted black, under the seats which worked as risers for the seats. Problem solved. Did I neglect to say that the previous owner's name was Shorty?

Next on the list was the engine compartment. Roger's A/C guy recommended Bobby who had a new system for heavy duty cleaning: "soda blasting." We went to see Bobby, who explained that his system, mounted on a trailer behind his pickup, would blast the engine compartment with baking soda which would clean everything down to bare metal and not damage anything. So we left the Widow at Bobby's house and said we would be back in the morning.

The following morning as we neared Bobby's house we noticed that the neighborhood houses and lawns appeared to be covered with a white film. The closer we got to Bobby's house the thicker the film appeared to be. Roger stated that it looked a lot like baking soda. We pulled into Bobby's driveway and saw the Widow, freshly washed and surrounded by what looked like 4 inches of snow. Bobby was standing next to the Widow with a garden hose in his hand. I look at the car and immediately notice that the interior is no longer black, **it's white**. Bobby says, with garden hose in hand, "I was just going to clean the interior."

"**No Bobby! No!** Put the garden hose down. We will take care of the interior." Bobby puts down the garden hose and goes over and opens the hood. And we see, in amazement, nothing but bare metal. The soda blasting really worked. It was clean as a whistle under the hood. Roger looks over at Bobby and says, "Did you happen to wash down the engine compartment with that garden hose?"

"Yesiree, I sure did, hosed her down real well." Roger's eyes roll and he tells me to get in and start the car. I slide into my new "white" interior, generating a white cloud of baking soda, and turn the key. The starter turns over but the car won't start. For the next two hours Roger wipes down everything in sight, especially the distributer, and I keep turning the key and listening to the starter grind away.

Soda Blasting Really Works!!!

Nothing works, so as a last resort I call my nephew Brian in New Jersey, a master mechanic, and explain the problem. After 10 minutes of Brian saying "You did **what** with baking soda?" we go through a 15 minute exercise of tests to isolate the problem. Brian finally comes up with the solution, "Sucker's broke!!" he says. "If it was a computer you'd have to re-boot. Cause it's a car, let it be over night, have a beer, and come back in the morning and try again." I have faith in Brian, as he has helped out many times before with car problems. Curiously all of Brian's solutions include, "have a beer", which I believe may be the key to his success. The next morning the Widow starts right up. I send Brian a

"Well Done" card and gift certificate for a case of Budweiser.

Getting Lucky...

My two week working vacation at Roger's was up and it was time to go back to Florida. The lawn needs mowing, the weeds need eating, and repair and maintenance opportunities abound. All will be taken care of...as soon as I get back from fishing.

Meanwhile back at Roger's, the Widow was having visitors. Word gets around quickly in White, Georgia. One of Roger's neighbors, Bud, stopped by to look at the Marauder. Bud is a Ford collector and has building after building filled with cars and parts. Bud liked the Marauder and offered to help out with any parts if he could. Roger had another neighbor and good friend, Brad, who owns Thunder Valley Customs. Thunder Valley is a top-of-the-line custom body and paint shop that has had multiple cars featured in Hot Rod and other magazines.

Thunder Valley Customs, White, Georgia

Wow... pretty neat neighborhood if you're a car guy!!!

News of the Marauder had gotten back to Brad and he showed up at Roger's to see this beast. Brad, like many people, had never seen a 69 Marauder X-100. So Roger told him all about it and Brad began looking over the car. He opened the doors, the trunk, and the hood and even crawled underneath it. As Brad walked around the car, his conversation with Roger turned to painting the car. Brad had an outstanding paint shop, but it was primarily for the custom cars that he built. Here's where I got really lucky!! Brad finally says, "I'll paint the car. You know I'm expensive, but you also know what kind of work I do."

After Brad leaves, Roger calls me with the news. I'm in shock; my Marauder is going into a top-of-the-line custom shop for paint ... *although top-of-the-line does seem a bit much for a daily driver car.* Roger begins to explain to me how well respected Brad is in the classic car world, telling me about some of the work he has done and the cars he has built and the magazines they have been in and....

Uh Oh!! *Logic whispers downs to me "Grab hold of something and hold on tight..."*

Roger continues, explaining that we have to strip the car of all of its trim, including bumpers and grille, before it goes into Brad's shop. Roger says if we do all of this then Brad will paint the car for only $5,000.

<u>**ONLY $5,000??**</u> *GASP!! GASP!! I can't breathe, there's no heart beat, I drop the phone... I'm a dead man!! How do I tell my wife that the cost of the paint job for my Marauder is almost as much as I paid for the car?* I take a deep breath, slowly pick up the phone, try to force a smile, and excitedly *(sniff)* tell Roger "That's great, Wow *(sniff)*. Oh Boy, I am so happy." *Sniff, sniff...*

I'm a dead man!!!

Actually, I am not a dead man. Severely crippled and sentenced to a life of perpetual agony, maybe!! In truth, my wife was very calm about it. It might have been the on-the-knees pose with tears cascading down my face that did it. She was very happy that I had an interest in this new hobby. She said the fact that it had gotten me out of my *retirement crisis*, was worth *almost* any amount of money.

So, relaxed and anxious, I was ready to go back to White, Georgia, and work on the Widow. A week later I fly to Atlanta and Roger meets me at the airport. On the ride back to his house he explains what we have to do to strip the car of its trim and get it ready for Brad. He also mentions that

I need to meet with Brad to settle everything first. Whoa!! I tell Roger that I thought that he had made all of the arrangements. He said he had but I needed to finalize everything with Brad. Finalize what? I am paying $ 5,000 (GASP!!) and Brad is going to paint the car black, end of story. Roger asks, "Is there anything you want Brad to do or not do? And what color black to you want?" I'm back into panic mode, "I just want it painted black! You know black, black-black!

"But there are many different blacks," notes Roger. I look for an escape route, a place to hide. Nothing!!! Finally I agree to meet with Brad.

WHY ME? *I'm not good at this face to face stuff, especially with strangers...*

The next day we go to Thunder Valley Customs. Brad is working on a copper colored 56 Chevy and waves to us. Roger escorts us through the shop pointing out Brad's creations. I am in awe. The workmanship is outstanding. The customization is creative and classily understated in an "I am unique, yet conservative" look. Not a radical "Bet you ain't seen anything like this (barf) look."

Brad finally comes over and I am introduced. Brad seems like a nice guy and shows us more of his shop. After a while I whisper to Roger, "You ready to go now?"

Roger says, "No, you need to go talk to Brad about your paint job."

"And say what!!" I reply.

GO!!! Roger says. "Okay, Okay," I mumble. I walk over to Brad and say "You're going to paint my car black, right?" Then I remember what Roger had said about there being many different blacks. So I quickly say, "Did you have a particular color

I have been set up!!!

of black in mind?"

Brad looks at me and says, "Not really, I have a 55 gallon drum of black out back, that okay??" I don't know what to say to this... and then laughter erupts throughout the shop. Brad and Roger are in hysterics and the rest of the shop is likewise. The "rookie" classic car owner has been initiated into the club, I have been set up, and the joke is on me. *I quickly look for a loose tire iron and...*

Actually it's pretty neat. I walked in as just a customer and now I've been accepted as one of the guys. After the laughter stops, Brad says not to worry, "I know what you want, I've talked to Roger, and you'll like it." Roger echoes that, and after handshakes all around we leave. *I think I might like this classic car stuff!!*

We go back to Roger's house and begin taking the trim off of the Widow. This takes a few days and a few muscles. The front bumper weighs more than me and the grille is in 10 different parts, with each attached to the other. The grille is like a puzzle: if you don't take each piece off in the correct order, you can't get them all off. We succeed, thanks to Roger, and give thanks it wasn't Toyota's engineers that designed it or we might still be there. We then attack the surface rust, which is minimal but boring. At last the Widow is naked and ready to go into Brad's shop.

The Widow is naked and ready to go for paint at Thunder Vally Customs

Before we can deliver the Widow to Brad he calls Roger with the bad news. As painting the Widow is a favor to

Roger, we do not have a priority in Brad's schedule. Brad apologies to Roger, but he has some top dollar work that has finally come in and he needs to concentrate on that first. The best estimate is 6 weeks before he can start on the Widow.

We have nothing to do now but wait, so I head back to Florida and leave the Widow with Roger. After about a week Roger calls me and says that the engine compartment, which Bobby soda blasted clean, is forming surface rust on the bare metal. Roger says we need to detail (paint) the engine and the engine compartment now. I tell Roger that I have a couple commitments this week but I can be up there next week. He says okay, but that he will start the task now before the rust gets any worse.

The following week there is an illness in the family and I need to go up to Pennsylvania for a while. The illness situation goes on for months. During this time Roger has finished the engine compartment and sends me pictures. Outstanding! It looks like a car right out of a showroom. As time passes in Pennsylvania the Widow goes into Brad's shop. Roger visits the shop periodically and sends me pictures of the work in process. Time continues to pass and the Widow comes out of Brad's shop and she is looking good. Roger and his wife, Leann, put all of the trim back on the Widow and Roger sends pictures. Wow!! Hard to believe this is the same car that was delivered to White, Georgia, six months ago.

ITS BEAUTIFUL

With the family issues finally resolved in Pennsylvania I get back to Florida and am greeted by many months worth of neglect on my property. Two weeks later the property is in a manageable condition and I fly up to Roger's. The ride from the airport to Roger's is one of anticipation. I need to see and drive my car. I need to get those 480 lbs. ft. of torque and 360 horsepower on the road. I even brought extra underwear. I am psyched!!!

We get to Roger's house and walk into his showroom and there she sits, a beautiful black beast. The paint is 3 feet deep and the body is perfect; in fact the entire car is perfect. Brad did the outside and Roger did the inside and the result is unbelievable. This is a car, a 1969 Mercury Marauder X-100, that most people have never even seen and it's sitting here in Roger's showroom in pristine condition, **and it's mine!!!** Roger lets me drool over the car for about 10 minutes, and then says we need to go see Brad so you can tell him if you're satisfied with his work. *Huh?*

The car is perfect, with the deepest black paint I have ever seen. Yeah, I'm satisfied. Okay, that's cool, let's go see Brad. I carefully get into my beautiful perfect car, turn the key, and the engine roars to life. I shift into reverse and prepare to back out of Roger's showroom, when I break out in a sweat. What if I scrape the side of the car backing out? I take a deep breath and slowly back out. My heart is racing, sweat pours out of me as I ease my perfect car out of the driveway. I slowly accelerate onto the highway careful not to spin the wheels and cause a stone or something to fly up and hurt my perfect car. My tee shirt is soaked, there's sweat in my eyes, and panic is setting in. *No!! No!! I'm afraid to drive my perfect car!!!*

Where is the muscle car I bought?? Where is my daily driver?? What will I do with all of that extra underwear I brought? My mind screams out, "Brad has destroyed my muscle car, he must pay!!!" I start to stomp on the gas, but back off quickly; I need to be careful with my perfect car. By the time we get to Thunder Valley Customs I am calmed down. Brad is with a customer when we arrive. He breaks free for a moment and I thank Brad for all he has done, assure him I am totally satisfied, and let him get back to his customer. Roger and I get in my perfect car and leave, driving slowly.

I am happy and I am sad. I am happy that I have this beautiful, rare car and a friend like Roger. I am happy to have been to White, Georgia, and met so many good people that helped make my introduction into the classic car arena an exciting and pleasurable experience.

I'm sad (actually, not really sad, but I don't know what the word is) that this experience is over and it's now a memory. I don't believe I will ever go through this again and I guess that's sad. But you never know. I am still in awe of my perfect car and I hesitate driving it. Roger says I will get over this, and Roger is the man, so I guess I will. Roger and I will head for my home in Bradenton tomorrow with the Widow on the trailer. Let's see, the Bradenton Drag Strip is open for timing runs on Thursday… **Hmm!! Might work!!!!**

That's how it happened…

That's how I got into the world of classic cars. I own a very rare 1969 Mercury Marauder X-100 in pristine condition that became a show car, with appearances at car shows throughout Florida, Concours d' Elegances, car magazines, and national television. Roger Papp restored this car to its perfect condition and Brad Cline, Thunder Valley Customs, put the icing on this cake. All of the praise and awards the car has received are directly attributed to their efforts. And of course, there's the Mercury Division of Ford Motor Company that built this magnificent beast.

I am just the owner…

And I did get over my fear of driving it. In fact, I take it out at least once a week, even looking around at stop lights for a little competition. It may be "show perfect" but it's still a muscle car and needs to be driven like one. And that's my story and I'm sticking to it!

Chapter 4
Backcountry Road Trip

The Author is forced to become an author by writing an article to get the Marauder in a national magazine...

When Roger and I first started looking for a muscle car, I searched through at least a thousand car ads trying to find *my* muscle car. I noticed that some ads made reference to the fact that the car had been featured in a national car magazine. The ad implied that this made the car special and consequently worth more money.

Hey! I can do this! I can make my Marauder more valuable! I will get it featured in a magazine! So off I went; sending emails with descriptions and pictures of my car to all of the classic car magazines. Most responded that they liked the car, and its rarity, and asked where the car was located. When I would respond that it was in Florida most came back saying I was too far away from their home office and they would not foot the expense of sending a photographer this distance. I offered to take the pictures but was told, politely (sometimes), that I was not a professional photographer. Hey! It wouldn't be my first picture (?), and it's a car magazine not National Geographic. I was not a happy camper and started looking for Guido's phone number.

Then, out of nowhere, Legendary Ford Magazine, which had already rejected me, came back and said that their editor liked the background on some of my pictures, specifically the oak trees with Spanish moss hanging down. Their magazine had a Road Trip section and they said that if I were to write an article, including pictures, for this section about a road trip into the back country of Florida they would include it in their magazine. Of course my car would be featured in this article.

Wow! My car is going to be in a national magazine! It will be famous! It will be valuable! All I have to do is write an article and ...and... Whoa!!! Write an article? Can I do that??? I had never written anything except business status reports, when I still worked for a living, so this was new, uncharted territory to me. I was eventually able to write and photograph a road trip article and the magazine actually published it.

Damn! I'm an Author!!!

This is an amended text version of that article *Road Trip...*

I'm a recently retired computer consultant who has spent the last 20 years traveling all over the world working primarily in third world countries. I was able to keep my sanity during this time because I would return home to Bradenton, Florida between trips. Bradenton is on the Gulf coast of Florida and has great weather, great fishing, great sunsets and great beaches. While not a beach guy I do live on the water, but it's backwater, with mangroves and lots of wildlife and not many people. It was instant therapy for a weary traveler like me.

I've lived in Florida for 25 years and with all of my traveling I haven't really seen much of the rest of Florida. My friend Earl, the guy who keeps my Marauder running, is a true Florida Cracker, (born and raised in Florida). We were talking the other day and Earl mentioned that he had taken his Mustang out to a car show in Arcadia, a little town about 45 miles inland. I had been in Arcadia only once, about 20 years ago. Earl made the cars, the people and the area sound really interesting. (It's unusual for Earl to make anything sound interesting, but I listened). It was a slice of old Florida he was talking about, and that's when we decided.

"*Road trip!*" We yelled in unison. (Well maybe not in unison! Still I am amazed that Earl and I actually thought alike on something). We decided to go on a road trip into the backcountry of Florida. Let me tell you a little about Earl. Earl is the ultimate classic car mechanic, body man, welder, etc., etc., but he is still a Florida Cracker. I am an ex-backyard mechanic that saw his better days back-in-the-day of Ford flatheads. Plus I'm an ex-northerner. So when Earl and I talk cars the harassment flows back and forth, Ace Florida Cracker Mechanic vs. Know-Nothing Northerner. Logically I win all of these arguments, but since logic is not relevant in any conversation with a Florida Cracker, I always lose! But it's all in fun and we're still friends.

Earl's idea for this road trip is that we will take my Marauder, use my gas and I would buy the meals. Earl, on the other hand, would ride shotgun as guide and interpreter, a position of importance, as Earl tells it, when you venture into the backcountry. Earl made some phone calls and soon we had a full day scheduled, with breakfast, lunch and dinner in different towns. Hopefully we will see some nice cars, do some sightseeing and taste the local cuisine. I said taste not eat. The local cuisine in the backcountry can be unique. I have tasted *hearts of palm* and smelled *swamp cabbage* but I can't truly say I have eaten either, or ever will.

Saturday morning 7 AM, I arrive at Earl's place. Earl looks eager and ready to go. Then I show him my new backcountry hat, Toby Keith style. His comments about my hat, while colorful and extremely specific are not really suitable for print. I decide against taking the hat along. It would be a long drive by myself. (See Ed lose, again! See Ed look for a tire iron--See Ed--Oh the hell with it)!

Hatless, but excited, I crank up the Marauder and we hit the road. The Marauder loves the cool morning air. Inhaling it down the massive 4-barrel, feeding all 360 horses as we cruise down the two-lane into the backcountry. Once out of civilization there are miles of farmland and cattle ranches bisected by manmade canals, that drain this swampland called Florida, to make it fit for man and beast. And beasts there be; bass and garfish in the canals; gators and water moccasins too; wild pigs rooting in the thickets and rattlesnakes sunning themselves on the rocks. Ain't it great!!!

Myakka City...

Our first stop is Myakka city. As we near the city the scenery suggests that we are now deep in the backcountry. I recall reading about a horse being attacked around here by what was believed to be a Florida Panther and I also recall the reported sighting of the *Myakka Skunk Ape,* a 7 foot ape that smells like a skunk. I mention these beasts to Earl and he is unimpressed with my newly found local knowledge. He says he knows people that have seen the Skunk Ape, but "they won't say nothing to nobody, cause they don't want to be laughed at." I tell him I find it hard to believe. He smiles and says, "Don't much matter now, there's a new beast in town," and our big black Marauder rolls into Myakka City.

Myakka City is a picturesque little town of about 4,000 that sits somewhere near the middle of nowhere. Its main claim to fame is the vast cattle ranches that surround it. It's also the winter home to the world famous Lipizzaner Stallions. *I'm not sure why.* We pull into the Ranch Restaurant.

I don't see any classic cars around. Earl refuses to tell me who or what we are meeting up with. He says, "It's a surprise." Earl has a surprise for me, now that's scary.

We just finish parking and I see this big car pull into the parking lot. Wow! It's a brother! A big black Mercury, a brother to my Marauder.   Earl says, "It's a 1972 Mercury Grand Marquis Brougham; I thought you'd like it. It belongs to Jimy Da Hook."

I say "What"? He explains that Jimy has a deformed index finger that is shaped like a hook. I ask if they actually call him that. He says that Jimy likes the name and even has a business card with Jimy Da Hook on it. "I'll get you one" he says. We meet Jimy and begin to look over his car. It is drop dead gorgeous, black on black and 100% original. His Grand Marquis is like a stately sophisticated brother to my bad boy Marauder.

We go into the Ranch restaurant, which I'm told is where the locals eat. Our waitress comes over and asks if we want the breakfast special. No one says a word so I finally ask, "What's the special?" She replies "Skunk Ape & Cheese Omelet." I've been had! (These Florida Crackers sure can be funny.) She then informs me that our breakfast order was called in ahead and would be ready in a few minutes. *Another surprise from Earl?*

Jimy tells us that he bought the Grand Marquis six years ago at the granddaddy of all cruises, the *Woodward Dream Cruise* in Detroit. The car had been in a museum for the previous 20 years and had 21,000 miles on it. We compare his Grand Marquis to my Marauder. His is heavier, longer and

plusher. *A real cruiser!* We both have 429 engines, mine has 360 HP but the *emissions gods* in 1972 reduced the Marquis' HP to 208. Just as Earl starts in about his Mustang, our food arrives. It's fried eggs, smoked mullet and grits. Great, I can handle this. And I do. The grits were actually quite good and the smoked mullet was, well, smoked mullet. Fish for breakfast! (Hey! Isn't that what the sophisticated British eat; only they call them kippers? Do you suppose that Florida Crackers are--nah-- no way?)

We shoot some pictures of Jimy's beautiful Grand Marquis. Jimy has to leave, so we part with our new friend and my Marauder's Marquis brother. Earl and I are left to explore Myakka City on our own. As we head toward Crane Park my thoughts briefly return to the Skunk Ape. (What if we see...)

Crane Park is the local campground and canoe launch on the Myakka River. The Myakka River is a dark ribbon of water that winds its way through the backcountry for some 30 miles until it finally reaches Charlotte Harbor and the green waters of the Gulf of Mexico. Anybody who thinks alligators are an endangered species should go canoeing on the Myakka River.

We reach Crane Park. It's beautiful, but also sort of eerie. It's quiet here, spooky quiet. You know that there are gators, rattlesnakes and moccasins within the sound of your voice, or closer. Wild pigs are around somewhere and maybe even a Panther or a Skunk Ape, and there are no fences or cages between them and us. The people that live here don't seem to care. Earl says "As far as the critters go, you leave them be, and they'll leave you be. At least most of the time," he adds. We take some photos, knowing there is no way we can really capture the beauty of this place on film. We just sort of hang out for a while, not saying much, just soaking it all in. We finally realize we have a schedule and have to get moving. Don't want to, but...we'll be back, stay longer, and maybe go canoeing (Earl's idea) among the endangered species. (*It had better be a big canoe...*)

Arcadia...

We leave Myakka City and head back down the two-lane toward Arcadia and deeper into the backcountry.

Arcadia, a town of 6600 situated in the in the Peace River Valley, is in the midst of rebuilding. In August of 2004, Hurricanes Charlie and Francis whipped up on Arcadia. Homes were destroyed, roofs ripped off, massive oak trees uprooted, and debris ended up everywhere. The winds were so severe they tore part of the roof off the town's hurricane shelter, with residents inside. The cattle industry was devastated from the widespread destruction of barns and other infrastructure. These people went through six weeks of hell, as four major hurricanes went around and through their city, yet they seem intent on rebuilding. It's still old Florida and their piece of Paradise. **Hurricanes be damned!!!**

The classic car population in Arcadia survived, many were damaged, but repairable, but none were destroyed. We were told of a classic car garage where the cars survived but an A/C unit in the back window blew out and flew across the garage and slammed into the front wall. A lot of the hurricane damage has been repaired but there are still homes with tarps on the roofs waiting to be repaired.

We were going to met Phil and his beautiful 428 CJ Mach 1. I met Phil at the All Ford Nationals at Bradenton Motorsports Park. I told Earl all about Phil's Mach 1 and he is anxious to see it, and to ask Phil for a ride. Just then the cell phone rings, it's Phil, he apologizes profusely as he explains that he can't meet us. He says that he has an *emergency of sorts*, but he has made arrangements for lunch and we should head for the Parker restaurant. Earl is devastated that he won't get a ride in the Mach 1. *And you ain't seen nothing until you've seen a devastated Florida Cracker! Not a pretty sight!* But magically the words *lunch* and *restaurant* register somewhere within Earl's devastation, and the recovery is swift.

We eventually find the restaurant and slide into a booth. A waitress comes over and says, "Is that your big black car out there."

We say, "Yes Ma'am." That makes us Phil's friends,

and we get a smile. She explains that Phil has called ahead and our meal will be right out. I ask what the meal is and I get another smile as she leaves. *Another surprise!* A man comes over and introduces himself as Bobby Joe, a friend of Phil's. He gives us a list of places to see and directions to get there. He then apologizes and says he can't join us, as he has an *emergency of sorts*. I think, *"What is going on with these 'emergency of sorts'? Is there something we should know?"* Then our lunch arrives.

It's Swamp Cabbage. I am afraid to ask if it's called Swamp Cabbage because it grows in the swamp or because it smells like a swamp. The next hour went by very slowly. If you want any details about our lunch you will have to ask Earl, as I refuse to talk about negative and humiliating things. As we finish eating, sort of, I explain to Earl that I have an *emergency of sorts* and head for some fresh air. Back outside I

rush to the bottle of mouthwash in the Marauder's glove compartment. *I seriously consider swallowing it all, but...* Earl and I check our Bobby Joe list and head out to Oak Street in downtown Arcadia. Oak Street is the historic district with large colorful brick buildings dating back to the first half of the 1900s. It's awesome, downtown old Florida. **COOL!**

Earl decides he wants a glass of milk. My stomach turns at the idea, but we stop at Brenda Lee's Café. Our tee shirts, with the car pictures on them, cause us to strike up a conversation with Denise and Larry who tell us they have a Car Museum some 11 miles north of Arcadia near Ona, Florida. They say they have a number of Fords and Mercurys including a 1929 Ford Doodlebug. I know a bit about Fords but can't place a Doodlebug. Larry explains that during World War II steel was scarce and many farmers couldn't afford tractors. So they converted their old cars into tractors. They kept only the engine, trans, rear and some sort of seat. They put two trannies back to back so when you put both in reverse, you had one really stump pulling low gear. Earl says, "I knew that." ***I really need to carry a tire iron!!!*** Larry is also an old drag racer and tells us about a little town near here where Saturday night you can always find some action at the local stoplights. He says it's safe as there are only 2 cops in town and you always know where they are. Earl's eyes light up at this. ***I think I can see the vacuum inside.*** Larry invites us up to the museum, which he says is still a mess from the hurricanes; he lost 42 feet of roof. It's been fixed but the inside hasn't been completely cleaned up yet. He has been working mostly on his other property damage. We explain that we have to meet someone but we would definitely take him up on his offer next trip. We thank Larry and Denise for the conversation and continue our walk through Arcadia.

We find the De Soto County Courthouse, Arcadia being the county seat, and it is a massive structure of old colonial architecture. Earl comments, "Ain't no hurricane gonna hurt that." As we return toward the car we see a flash of bright yellow on a side street. We walk toward it and it is a 1941 Ford Street Rod. It's parked next to Wheeler's Café.

...ain't no hurricane gonna hurt that.

We go inside, my stomach has recovered, I think, and find out the street rod belongs to Chuck, the owner of the café. Earl and I order Wheeler Burgers and talk cars with Chuck. He tells us that down the road apiece is a building where he has nine other Fords and Mercs of various years. He invites us to go down and see them but we decline and take a rain check as we do have to leave. As we leave Earl and I agree we will be back to see Chuck's cars and Larry and Denise's "Tin Memories" car museum. It's been interesting, and the people have been great in Arcadia. I can see why they are rebuilding and not leaving. It is definitely a piece of Paradise.

LINGER LODGE...

On the road again, we point the Marauder toward the southeast corner of Manatee County. We are going to meet up with Bob and his 1954 Mercury at Linger Lodge. Linger Lodge has been around since forever, which in Florida time is around 1940. It was originally a fishing camp on the headwaters of the Braden River. It's now an RV park and a restaurant. The Owner, Frank, was a taxidermist and over the years has filled the walls and ceiling with stuffed animals and reptiles. Many were road kill while others were the direct result of self-defense. Speaking of reptiles, that's why we're here. The Lodge reportedly serves up the best alligator in the state.

As we pull into the Lodge, Bob, his gorgeous Mercury  and a crowd of spectators are waiting for us. The Mercury hardtop, with its continental kit really draws a crowd. *I hope someone notices the Marauder...* The Lodge is not very impressive as you pull in, except for maybe the hay bales stacked by the entrance. Bob, Earl and I quickly agree to postpone the photo shoot until after we've had some gator. As we go inside, a 12 foot gator with a human leg in its mouth stares at us. I'm sure it's stuffed... **Now I'm impressed.** The  walls and ceiling are covered with wildlife, 50 plus years of taxidermy. The dining area and deck overlook the dark waters of the Braden River. You can see where a family of wild pigs has rooted up part of the riverbank. That's old Florida out there. COOL!!

Our waitress tells us, "Ya'all got a choice of Cajun or honey mustard gator." In some circles this might be cause for some decision-making. Not us, "We'all will have both." As we wait, the talk turns to cars and the taxidermy specimens on the walls and ceiling. The biggest attention getter is the overhead portion of the bar. Twenty five rattlesnakes of various sizes in various positions line the area just above the bar stools. In one section the rattlesnakes actually spelled out "Linger Lodge." COOL!!!

Apparently the waitress had seen our type before, as when our dinner arrives it's in three individual portions, thus eliminating a gruesome scene of hands flying across the table grabbing at food. In Florida Cracker that's "Grab your'en before he grabs his'en." Before I can dig in, Earl asks if I've, "Ever et Cajun gator." I say no, and then he warns me, "Watch out for the toenails, they're sharp and crunchy." No one laughs, but I know it's a put on. *I really really should carry a tire iron!!* When no one is looking I work over my portion of gator with a fork, looking for sharp crunchy things, can't be too safe.

Dinner over and full of gator we go check out Bob's ride. The Mercury is looking good, not too many of these cars left. Bob's a quiet unassuming guy, but get him started on his Mercury and you quickly understand what true love is. Bob tells the story of how he has always wanted a classic Mercury, but other priorities kept taking the funding away from his dream. As Bob's wife, Dot, tells the story, she was *forced* by her sister to go with her to a gambling casino. While there, Dot won a big chunk of money. When she got home she told Bob what she had won and that the money was his... to buy his dream Mercury. ***Is that cool or what!!!*** I think back on how I got my classic Mercury... ***nope it wasn't like that.***

Bob bought a 1954 Mercury hardtop that was in nice shape but needed some work, and Bob had ideas for some minor customization to make it his dream car. But again, funding was going to other priorities and the Merc sat. The most noticeable problem with the Merc was the typical *faded paint on the roof*. After some months of looking at the roof of the Merc through the kitchen window, Dot decided to do something about it. While Bob was at work she went out to the Merc with some Brillo Pads and began sanding the roof. When this didn't seem to help, she got some spray paint and applied that to the roof. She wasn't happy with the result, but she thought it looked better than it did before. When Bob got home from work, he saw what Dot had done... After *admiring* Dot's effort... *for a fairly long time*... Bob went into the house.

Now, those of you who that "have had" their wives paint the roofs of their classic cars (with a spray can) can probably imagine how the conversation between Bob and Dot went. For those few of you that "haven't had" this happen to you <u>yet</u>, this is how it went. Bob thanked Dot for her efforts and told her that she had done the right thing. It was he that had waited too long; it was time to redo the Merc. And the rest is history.

Earl and I finish our photo shoot; thank Bob for his good company, invite him to have dinner with us again at Linger Lodge and to please bring Dot with him. As Bob drives off in his beautiful Mercury, Earl comments on what an awesome couple Bob and Dot are. This is probably the first time I have ever completely agreed with Earl, and I wholeheartedly did. We start to head for the Marauder when a gorgeous red Torino pulls into the parking lot. Earl says, "That's Dwain and his 1969 Torino GT, he wasn't sure if he was going to make it."

Earl introduces us and immediately says to Dwain, "Ed's buying desert; River Bottom Pie for everyone." I guess it's dessert before everything when someone else is buying. "*In Florida Cracker World it sure is.*" I guess checking out Dwain's ride can wait. We stampede back into Linger

Lodge with Earl screaming out "River Bottom Pie all around." Well River Bottom Pie looks exactly like a backcountry Florida river bottom, dark brown and muddy. Surprisingly, I now have a new favorite backcountry food, besides gator. River Bottom Pie is a mixture of sinfully rich chocolate, caramel, Oreos and ice cream. Sinfully good! *I feel like I need to say 10 Hail Marys.* Earl hands me the check and says, "Hurry up and pay so we can check out Dwain's Torino." *He wouldn't say that if I was carrying a tire iron!*

Outside, Dwain's Torino brings back memories, as back-in-the-day I owned a yellow 68 Torino GT. As we look at the Torino, it's easy to see that when it comes to detailing a car, I am not in the same league as Dwain. Dwain tells of weeks of crawling under the Torino with a scraper and a wire brush cleaning the underbody of the Torino so it could be detailed. We look underneath the car and it looks better than the topside of most cars. You could eat gator off the underside, even the toenails. We talk for a while and shoot some pictures and then Dwain has to leave, dinner is waiting at home for him. Hope the River Bottom Pie hasn't ruined his appetite.

Earl and I walk down to the dock behind Linger Lodge and enjoy the beauty of the Braden River. The backcountry of Florida is a total contradiction to the seashores and hotel lights of the coast. It's a quiet peaceful part of the world with small patches of civilization surrounded by nature and wildlife. The critters were here first, and as long as the people that live here think that way everything is fine. I

guess it's time for us to leave the backcountry to the critters and get back to our civilization.

As we leave Linger Lodge we realize this is a one of a kind place. Nothing else like it exists anywhere; not in Florida; not in the US; not anywhere. A lot of Old Florida is disappearing as developers clear and pave the backcountry. Progress, or concrete, pushes on. Here's hoping that Linger Lodge survives. Earl and I are thankful for all that has happened today. It's been a great trip through just a little piece of Old Florida. And this is just the beginning. There's the Everglades, Lake Okeechobee, the Panhandle, so many places we haven't been and so many classic cars we haven't lusted over. **We point the Marauder directly at a beautiful full color sunset and start heading on home. Just another day in paradise!** "It doesn't get any better than this. See ya'all next trip."

Chapter 5
Last train to Twitsville
The Author encounters the ruling body of the Classic car World and lives to tell about it (barely)...

PART 1.

The ACCA...
Before we start I need to tell you that this story has nothing to do with trains. Also Twitsville may or may not exist. Good start, huh?

This story is about the American Classic Car Association (ACCA) and my relationship with them. Let's get this out up front: I DON'T UNDERSTAND THEM AND

THEY DON'T UNDERSTAND ME. First, let me say that the ACCA is the premiere classic car organization in the world and they have done many fantastic things for the classic car community since the early 1900s. They are to be commended for this.

Unfortunately they are still back in the early 1900s. The '50s and '60s appear to be an alien culture to them. In the '50s we all customized our cars: nosed, decked, skirts, etc. That was our thing. In the '60s it was muscle cars and performance. We still customized, but it was our engines not our cars. Some of us *souped up* our cars; others just put chrome goodies under the hood. *We made them our cars, our personalities, something different, not our father's cars, not the factory's cars.* They were *our cars.* The ACCA frowns upon this, or any rebellion of individualism. "*The Factory* is God" they say. "*The Factory* hath built it like this, therefore it is righteous and *thou shalt not modify.*" More on this later!

Growing up in the '50s and '60s, I nosed and decked numerous Fords, even put Turnpike Cruiser skirts on one during the '50s. The '60s got me into muscle cars like a 409 Impala SS, 440 Charger R/T, Chrysler 300, Torino GT, etc. My muscle cars were engines with wheels. Good looking wheels,

1969 Charger R/T 440 4-speed　　　1963 Impala SS 409 4-speed

but mostly engines. In the '60s, going to the local drive-in meant opening your hood and showing off your engine. A clean engine, with chrome goodies made you *The Man*. Well, *The Man* got married and had a family. I became a soccer and Little League Dad. No more muscle cars. My *car thing* became driving kids to games in SUV's with dirty engines. This was the life I followed while my family grew up. Don't get me wrong, I loved it. But back in some remote part of my brain *The Man* lived on.

OK, back to the subject of this story: the ACCA and me.

My Story...

After the Marauder was out of the paint shop at Thunder Valley Customs there were only a few minor tweaks here and there to get it to a finished *original* state. Roger had done an outstanding job on the car and in particular the engine compartment. You could eat off the Ford blue air cleaner and valve covers.

As I was admiring Roger's workmanship, *The Man* suddenly emerged from some recess deep in my brain. His first and only word to me was **"CHROME"**. I knew what he meant and I told Roger that we needed to go down to the auto parts store to get some chrome valve covers and a chrome air cleaner. As I started for the car, Roger stepped in front of me and made the sign of the cross (I learned later that it was actually an 'A' for ACCA). He said, "You can't do that. They will be upset." I said, "Who will be upset." He said, "The ACCA".

I said, "Huh?"

Roger explained to me that the ACCA was the *governing body* that ruled the classic car hobby. If I put chrome under the hood of this car then it would no longer be "factory original." I said, "Huh?" again. Roger explained that the ACCA believes that the "factory", (GM, Ford, Chrysler, etc) are a supreme deity, and that the perfection that they produced from their assembly line should "never" be modified, added to, or deleted from. Consequentially, if I were to "modify" the car and put chrome under my hood and then were to enter it into an ACCA car show (the only car shows that mattered, I was told) then the ACCA would deduct thousands of points from my score, and I would come in last, to a chorus of ridicule from thousands of ACCA members throughout the world.

Meanwhile *The Man* continued to yell out to me from that recess in my brain, "YOU HAVE A '60S CAR. IF THIS WAS THE 1960s YOU WOULD BE RIDICULED IF YOU DIDN'T PUT CHROME UNDER THE HOOD. IT'S A NATURAL THING. IT MUST BE DONE." All the while Roger continued to extol the virtues of the ACCA and *The Factory* as I nodded in agreement. *The Man* and Roger continued to whack away at me, *The Man* with passion, and Roger with pure logic. When Roger finished I was forced to agree with him, and pleaded for his forgiveness. Then as I saw him relax, I grabbed the keys and jumped into the Mercury and headed for the parts store. Some hours later I returned with my chrome masterpiece under the hood.

Chrome Masterpiece

I showed it to Roger, and, as always, he understood. He looked at me and said, "You are what you are. You are *The Man*." To further establish my status as *The Man* I showed Roger the tach and gauges that had sprouted up on my steering column. "Man does not live by idiot lights alone", *The Man* proudly explained (at least not with a 40 year old car).

Roger and I continued to go round and round about the ACCA. Actually, that only happened when I made unkind remarks about the ACCA. My bad! After many discussions with Roger I decided that 'A' 'C' 'C' 'A' is difficult to say when you are mad and talking fast and loud. So I came up with TWITS (Tightly Wound Inflexible Twerps) to replace ACCA. Now, no matter how mad or how loud I got, it was easy to say things like, "Those damn TWITS."

Now, Roger and I are normally in agreement about most things. When we disagree, Roger normally just considers the source and puts up with me. But when he feels I go overboard, like he felt I did with the TWITS, Roger will smack me in the face with "logic." Like he did here:

Roger: "Have you ever been to an ACCA Car Show?"
The Man: "Er, no."
Roger: "Then how do you know so much about them?"
The Man: "Er... Er..."

So that's when I reluctantly agreed to take the Mercury to Twitsville. I would go to an ACCA Car Show. As luck would have, Roger pointed out that there was one scheduled 2 weeks from now, only 50 miles away. I would go there, but, *The Man* would go fully dressed, with chrome under the hood and gauges gleaming on the steering column.

Part 2.

Showtime...

As I hope you have noticed, there are no trains in this story. I know what the title says, but really, there are no trains.

I spent the next 2 weeks getting the Mercury ready for the show. One week detailing the car, and one week polishing the chrome goodies. I was ready!

On the day of the show I was nervous as I pulled into the registration area. One of the smiling TWITS came out to greet me and immediately spotted the gauges on my steering column. He quickly backed off making the sign of the cross, uh; I mean the sign of the 'A'. He huddled with a small group of TWITS and came back to the Mercury and informed me that I was in 'Q' Class, and to follow the golf cart to the parking area. I asked what 'Q' Class is, and was sternly told "IT IS 'Q' CLASS!!!"

As I followed the golf cart for what appeared to be miles, we reached 'Q' Class parking at the very end of the car show grounds. A few of the 'Q' Class parking spots were already taken by a 1980 Yugo, two John Deere tractors and a dumpster. The next 5 hours were spent in discussion with my fellow 'Q's. The Yugo guy pretty much stayed to himself looking at a map, apparently unsuccessfully trying to find Yugoslavia, and the Yugo Service center. The John Deere guys were extremely animated in explaining to me the superiority of John Deere green over British Racing green. The dumpster just took it all in.

A few of the "Q" Class parking spots were taken...

At last, the moment arrived. The judge was here. I began to sweat. He spent about 5 minutes each, inspecting the Yugo, and the two John Deere tractors, and a good 15 minutes on the dumpster. My turn finally arrived!!!

The questions started:

TWIT judge: "Are these new tires?"

The Man: "The old ones wore out."

TWIT Judge: "Do you have factory air?"

The Man: "Yes, it is original factory A/C."

TWIT Judge: "NOT A/C!!! Do you have factory air in the tires?"

He could tell by looking at me that I was confused, so he knelt down and sniffed the valve stem on one of my tires. As he sniffed, he explained that when the tires were changed I should have bled the factory air out, saved it, and then put it back into the new tires. Dumbfounded, I asked how he could tell it wasn't factory air. Trying to eliminate those details that a layman such as I couldn't possibly understand, he stated "I am a highly trained ACCA professional judge." I was impressed and asked how he got himself into such an important position. He said it was a natural progression from his professional career as a Wal-Mart greeter. *I nodded, fully understanding*.

Satisfied that I was suitably impressed, he made a note on his judge's sheet and turned to inspect the engine compartment. My chrome masterpiece, in all of its glory, gleamed out at him. He froze for a split second and then made a move I couldn't believe a man his age could make. In a single motion he leaped backward through the air, simultaneously making the sign of the "A" while pulling a 12 inch red marking pen out of his back pocket. Eyes gleaming like black coals he started back toward my engine compartment, the red marker swishing through the air like Zorro's sword. Within slashing distance of my chrome goodies he suddenly stopped. His face turned white but he quickly composed himself, much like a Wal-Mart greeter would while watching a redneck hiding a flat panel TV under his shirt bolt from the store. He then made a Zorro like slash with the red marker on his judge's sheet and he was gone…

Time for me to be gone!!! I looked around and all of the exits have cars blocking them. I turn to my fellow 'Q's for help but they are shielding their eyes from me and talking to the dumpster. This is not going well. The loudspeaker announces that the awards are next, right after 2 ½ hours of raffle prizes. The awards finally start and go on for 2 hours. Finally the 'Q' Class awards come up. The dumpster wins 3rd place. I learn there are no 1st or 2nd places in 'Q' Class. They announce that 2 more awards remain. The Best-of-Show award goes to a '69 Mustang that had what appeared to be price tags and chalk markings on every part of the car. It looked like the classic car version of Minnie Pearl, only funnier. The TWITS erupt in unison at the proclamation of this Grand TWITS winner.

The last award, I hear over the loudspeaker, is the Worst-of-Show. Dead silence falls over the TWITS, followed by an uneasy rumbling among the crowd. The loudspeaker howls out my name, thunder crashes and lighting flashes as the sky goes dark and my Mercury is surrounded by flames. I shudder as an ominous chant slowly rises up from the mass of TWITS. I watch as they put on white hoods and pull out Ballantine Beer can openers, the ones capable of scratching an inch deep into chrome and paint. The chant gets louder, as making the sign of the 'A', the hooded TWITS move toward my Mercury.

PANIC!!!   WHERE AM I???   I realize that I'm home, in bed, in the fetal position lying in a pool of sweat. It was a dream! Thank goodness!

Or was it an omen??

PART 3.

The Real Deal...

In case you forgot!! There are no trains in this story. Just try to hang in there with me, we are almost there.

On the day of the show I was nervous as I pulled into the registration area. It was *déjà vu* all over again, I thought. Only this time it's for real. As I was sitting in line, Bill, a guy I knew from many car shows came over, said hello and asked if he could help with the registration. I showed him what I had filled out and he said he would take care of it. Nice guy, I didn't know he was in the ACCA. They're being nice. Damn!

"Don't trust them," *The Man* yells out from that recess in my brain. By the time I get the car up to the registration desk everything was taken care of. The Mercury was qualified for two different classes, Classic Ford and Ford Muscle. The guys at the registration desk said it was my choice but they felt that I shouldn't be with the muscle cars. As *The Man* and I were about to question why I shouldn't be with the muscle cars, one of them said, "That's a beautiful classic car. It belongs with the Classic Fords." Others echoed agreement. I said OK.

This being nice stuff is seriously damaging my story. But the judging hadn't started yet. I had all my under-hood chrome shined up and my gauges stood out like spotlights on the Mercury's steering column. I was ready for the judges.

I was actually having a good time. There were some outstanding cars in my class and the other car owners proved to be good guys and the day went fast. The highlight/lowlight of the day was the stalker. At least I think he may be a stalker. This is the same guy that I have seen many times before at local car shows, always taking pictures of the Mercury and telling me that he saw me on American Muscle Car TV. He is here now, standing in front of me and he says he wants my picture with the Mercury. This is weird. The guys I am sitting next to are staring at him and me, and he is acting like he is not going away until I say OK. I reluctantly agree and he takes my picture in front of the Mercury. He is happy, and I am worried. He leaves and I take a significant amount of crap about this from the other car guys.

As the day wears on I keep meeting guys that I knew from other car shows and find out that they are ACCA members. I had thought they were nice guys. The show is a packed house of car guys and spectators, both saying nice things about the Mercury. This is cool!!

As I walk around the car show I notice a large area full of Street Rods. Whoa!! I'm all original with just a few chrome goodies under my hood; these are fully customized cars that are all chrome under the hood. Did they sneak in, force their way in, or did I walk through some kind of a time warp? I talk to them and they tell me that ACCA is changing, and one of the changes is creating classes for Street Rods. I ask if the TWITS know about this. I get blank looks. My bad!

Whoa!! A large area full of street rods. Do the TWIT's know about this??

I head back toward my car trying to sort things out in my mind. Street Rods, nice people, having a great time, etc. What happened to the TWITS? Where are they? I demand to know. With *The Man* screaming this in my brain, the Classic Ford owners go suddenly quiet...

Here come the judges. Now we get down to it, *The Man* is ready! There were 2 of them going over, in tedious detail, each of the cars in my class. One of them seemed somewhat normal, very old and very businesslike. The other was exactly how you would picture a grumpy old man. He was intense and frowning as he inspected each car. After he finished going through the Mercury and moved on to the next car, I went to close the Mercury's trunk. As I did, I noticed he was looking back at the Mercury. I thought, *Oh crap, here it comes.* I said, apologetically, "I thought you were finished." He said he was finished; he was just looking at the nice lines of the Mercury with the trunk closed.

Returning nice for nice, I asked him, "How do you do this judging with all of these nice cars. It must be hard?"

He said it was. "Most of the cars are pretty equal, it comes down to a bolt not painted here, a scratch there, etc." I was ready to hit him with "*How about chrome goodie's, like under my hood?*" when he said "There are some things you don't penalize for, like this car over here. It has four Magstar wheels but the spare in the trunk has a hubcap on it. It was done to make the car look nicer, no harm in that. He didn't modify the car and I'm not going to penalize him for that." I am beginning to like this grumpy old man. **DAMN!!!**

The loudspeaker finally announces that it is time for the awards. Great, I'm a bit tired. But first, the loudspeaker announces, we have 2 hours of raffle tickets. Uh Oh! It is *déjà vu* all over again. Two hours later the raffle finally ends, I haven't won anything. I guess I should have bought some tickets.

Finally the awards start. The Classic Ford class is one of the first ones announced, and the Mercury wins 2nd in Class. **Huh!!** I begin moving toward the trophy presenters, while *The Man* screams at me, **"I HAVE CHROME GOODIES UNDER MY HOOD AND GAUGES ARE GROWING ON MY STEERING COLUMN; YOU CAN'T DO THIS".** I am forced to ignore *The Man* and I accept the trophy with gracious thanks, and to kind applause from the other car owners.

What's going on here? I try to reconcile with *The Man*. What happened to

YOU CANT DO THIS!!!

Twitsville, *The Man* and I scream out to each other? Is this another dream? Is the ACCA really just a bunch of car guys, or are they the TWITS we know and love?

My guess is that they are a group that is changing with the times, maybe not fast enough for me, but that's my problem. They are living by rules, very strict rules for their National Shows. But they honor these rules, can't blame them for that. I can blame them for not changing more of the rules, and faster. Or I can blame myself for sitting back and complaining and not doing something about it.

Or better yet, I can blame Roger and call him a TWIT. He'll just let the words bounce off until he decides to smack me in the head again with that logic stuff.

Maybe the last train to Twitsville has left the station. Maybe there is no Twitsville? Maybe there's a different destination, the new ACCA. In any case, if I find out which is which, I'll let you know, after I talk to *The Man* of course.

Ford Blue on the Wall

Oh, by the way, when I got back home from the ACCA Show and was standing in my garage thinking about the day's activities, *The Man* emerged again from that little recess back in my brain. He said two words to me, very softly: "Ford Blue." I knew what he meant and I went to get the original Ford Blue air cleaner and valve covers down from the wall. *Roger will be proud of me.*

Oh yeah, if any of you have any questions about the trains in this story, please go to my web site **www.aint-no-trains-dummy.com**.

Chapter 6
Local Car Shows

Way more than you would ever want to know about local car shows. Satire or truth? You be the judge...

My experience with the ACCA whetted my appetite for car shows. So I began looking for shows to take my Marauder to. Fortunately, living in Florida, there were local car shows pretty much every weekend, year around, within a 30 mile radius of where I lived. The first local car show I took my Marauder to, it won a trophy. ***Pretty cool!!*** I quickly became addicted. Of course I find out later that virtually everyone that brings a car to a local car show for the first time gets a trophy. It's like the local drug dealer giving you a free taste to get you hooked. Well, I was hooked. I began cleaning and polishing the car for all I was worth. I attended all of the local, and not so local, car shows I could, and I won trophies at most. When I didn't win a trophy it was easy to figure out that the low-life judge had it in for me, or there was some funny stuff going on. This compulsion for trophies lasted about a year. During that year, many times I contemplated calling cousin Guido in New Jersey and giving him the address of a judge.

My revelation on trophies came while I was complaining to a long time classic car collector about how I was robbed of a trophy by the stupidity, or possible criminal actions, of a Neanderthal judge. The car collector looked at me and offered these words of wisdom that I will never forget. He said, "**GROW THE HELL UP!!!**" I did… and I thank him for it. *Unfortunately, as I will explain later, not all of the car owners at car shows have benefited from these words of wisdom.* I finally realized that local car show judges are just people. They have favorites, prejudices, good days, bad days and those days that they are just trying to make it through the day. I applaud them. I couldn't do it. I have all of the human failings they do, *and more*.

Now, let's discus exactly what a local car show is. There are 5 basic requirements for a car show.
1. Classic cars & their owners
2. Spectators
3. '50s music and a Disc Jockey to play the music.
4. Door Prizes
5. Trophies.

CLASSIC CARS & THEIR OWNERS…

Most classic car shows restrict the cars by their age. It can be something like, "must be 20 years old or older," or, "must have been built prior to 1973." Some car shows have no restrictions and allow newer cars. The shows that allow new cars can really irk *Classic Car Guy*. As an example: you can have a 1969 Camaro that *Classic Car Guy* took 4 years to painstakingly and lovingly restore, parked next to a brand new Chrysler 300 SRT8 that its owner paid $50,000 for yesterday. Both are nice cars, but these two owners are not compatible. *Classic Car Guy* aches to (sarcastically) ask *New Car Buyer Guy* how long it took him to restore his car, but he doesn't. Also *Classic Car Guy* loves the '50s music playing in the background, but he can't hear it since *New Car Buyer Guy* has his stereo cranked up and is pounding out heavy metal music. Add that to the fact that *New Car Buyer Guy* has no idea what a "Wooly Bully" is, and he doesn't care.

While it appears that I am defending *Classic Car Guy*, *which I am,* there are two different *Classic Car Guys*. *Classic Car Restorer Guy* spent 4 years lovingly restoring his 69 Camaro. *Classic Car Buyer Guy* also has a 69 Camaro, which he just bought for $50,000 from a different *Classic Car Restorer Guy* who had spent 4 years lovingly restoring it. Throw in the possibility that *Classic Car Buyer Guy* and *New Car Buyer Guy* both spent years saving their money so they could buy the car of their dreams and you really confuse the issue. *I guess what it all boils down to is that all of these car owners love their own cars, but many have no idea why the other guy loves his.*

So we have the *Classic Car Restorer Guy*, the *Classic Car Buyer Guy* and the *New Car Buyer Guy*. Sounds like this conflict might be the major social problem at local car shows, right? **Wrong, Kemo Sabe!!!** It is *nothing* compared to the conflict between GM owners (primarily Chevy), Ford Motor Co. owners (primarily Ford), Chrysler/MOPAR owners (primarily all of them) and the Independents or Orphans like Studebaker, American Motors, Hudson, etc.

The *Chevy Guys* have a dominance of numbers at most shows and believe that this means they are special. The *Ford Guys* are a minority and so believe they are special. The

MOPAR Guys believe that since most classic MOPAR cars have rusted out and disappeared, their rareness makes them special. The *Orphan Guys* have no idea what is going on and don't care.

Even these groups have factions within themselves. The *Chevy Guys* have the *Corvette Guys* as an elite group within. *Corvette Guys* know that they are elite because you can't be more elite than being grown men driving little plastic cars. The *Ford Guys* have the *Mustang Group* within.

Plastic Car!

This is the *Mongolian Horde* type group that numbers in the gazillions. There are so many Mustangs that the Mustang car shows are forced into many, many classes, like all red 1966 Mustangs with A/C and a lighted ash tray might be in one class (of course limited to the first 100 entrants). The *Mustang Guys* are also a religious group, devoutly worshipping the God *"Shelby."*

One of a Gazillion???

The *MOPAR Group* is so small they have no internal groups. They may not even be a group, just individuals worshipping at the altar of the God *"Hemi."* The *Orphan Group's* internal groups outnumber the group itself.

OK, so now we understand what the major social problems at car shows really are, right? **Wrong again, Kemo Sabe!!** This is nothing. The *Classic Car Guys* with their Chevys, Fords, MOPARs and Orphans will band together at a moment's notice when a *Street Rodder Guy* or *Custom Car Guy* appears.

Classic Car Guy believes in saving the past by restoring or owning a car that is factory original, or very close to that. The *Ultimate Classic Car Guy* has a car that is original down to the tags and chalk markings that the factory put on the cars while on the production line. This *Ultimate Classic Car Guy* is commonly referred to in the classic car community as the *Doofus*. **But I digress.** *Classic Car Guy* believes that *Street Rodder Guy*, with his hacksaw and welding torch, has destroyed the beauty and originality that the automotive factories produced on their assembly lines. History has been destroyed, and that cannot be forgiven.

Street Rodder Guy believes that the automotive factories produced cars for the masses. While these cars were original, they had no real originality. *Street Rodder Guy* believes he is an artist and that he transforms these mass transit vehicles into works of art, defining for the world to see his true being. OK, so this must be the major social problem at car shows, right? ***You better believe it!!*** North vs. South, Romans vs. Huns, Sylvester vs. Tweety Pie; this is the tie that doesn't bind. But, with all of that, they all still show up, park next to each other and stand in the registration line together. Then they run to their own little Car Guy groups and talk smack about the other Car Guy groups.

While *Classic Car Guy* and *Street Rodder Guy* vie for the Best of Show, they have no chance at all. Ninety nine percent of *Classic Car Guy's* cars are driven to the local car shows. They are driven because they are cars, and *Classic Car Guy* loves to drive his car. But there is that 1% of cars that arrive at the shows on trailers. These are the *Trailer Queens*. Some are actually *driven* off the trailer for the show, but that is rare. Most are pushed off the trailer and then pushed in place for the show. *Trailer Queen Guy* is unique in that he has the "car gene" missing from his DNA. It has been replaced with the "statue gene" which radiates "don't touch it," "don't move it," and, "give me trophy" waves to his brain. *Trailer Queen Guy*

dreams of having a hurricane proof, solid glass, environmentally controlled trailer so he doesn't have to expose his car to the outside world. *Classic Car Guy* dreams of a *Trailer Queen-free world*.

A large percentage of Trailer Queens are owned by *Classic Car Collector Guy*. I met my first *Classic Car Collector Guy* some 3 years ago at a local car show. I was admiring his 61 Galaxie Starliner and he told me that it was an exact copy of a '61 he owned back-in-the-day. I commented that wouldn't it be great if you could own now, all of the cars you used to own back-in-the-day. He said, "**I do.**" and then told me about the gazillion square foot building that housed his cars. It was spread over 3 counties just north of Tampa and is so large that the building has 15 zip codes. His spare parts alone have 4 different zip codes. I saw him only that one time, never again. Rumor has it that he is lost in one of the spare parts zip codes never to be seen again. It is believed that *Classic Car Collector Guy* lacks the, "sharing gene" in his DNA which has been replaced by the "its mine" and "lock it up" genes. A common malady that affects *Classic Car Collector_Guy* as he gets older is the "Museum Virus" which destroys the "lock it up" gene. Symptoms of the *Museum Virus* are an urge to sell tickets and add the word Museum to the end of his name.

Then there is the unpredictable *Classic Car Gal*. She may show up in a stock pink Mustang, or a '50s Street Rod pickup, or in a 600 HP T-Bird. There is no rhyme or reason to her cars. *Classic Car Gal* is normally quiet and keeps to herself. After all she is a definite minority in this ocean of testosterone. *Classic Car Guy* keeps his distance from *Classic Car Gal* as *Classic Car Guy Wife* is very hostile to *Classic Car Gal*. *Why is she here? Where is her husband? Is she after my Classic Car Guy? Does she charge by the hour?*

As each *Classic Car Gal* arrives at a show there is an immediate meeting called of the *Classic Car Guy Wives* to classify and determine the impending threat from this misplaced female. *Classic Car Gal* reacts to all of this attention or non-attention with a polite smile. A sure indication of her evil motives, notes *Classic Car Guy Wife*.

SPECTATORS...

A local car show cannot exist without spectators. They are the fuel that keeps the car shows running. While *Classic Car Guy* will tell you he is there for the camaraderie of his fellow *Classic Car Guys, which he is*, more likely he is there to have his classic car adored by the worshipping spectators. A classic car show is no different than any artist's gallery where the artist shows off his work. The cars are works of art and *Classic Car Guy* is the artist.

The spectators are as different as the *Classic Car Guys* are. There is the *"I used to own one of those"* spectator who back-in-the-day used to own a car like *Classic Car Guy's* car. Sometimes it was the exact car, sometimes a variation of the car, and sometimes not so much the same car. As an example of "not so much the same car" I was parked next to a friend that had a 1969 yellow Camaro convertible. A spectator came up and said to my friend, "I used to own one of those." The conversation, heavily one-sided in the spectator's favor, continued for a while as the spectator detailed the history of *his car,* including the fact that his was blue, and it was a 4 door, and it was a 1974, and it was a Buick.

Then there is the *I Got Pictures* spectator. He approaches and says, "Nice car you got there." And before you can thank him for his kind words he pulls out pictures of his car, a 1985 Chevy station wagon, and proceeds to describe in detail its history, his history and his family's history. This can be extremely lengthy and many times only an, "Excuse me, I gotta go..." can end it. Hopefully when you do go, he doesn't follow you.

Then there is *"The Expert"* spectator. He walks past each car in the show explaining to his wife/girlfriend what each make and model is, and its history. As I sit next to my 1969 Mercury Marauder I can hear him explaining that my car is a 1956 Riviera, an Oldsmobile luxury car that they raced in NASCAR.

Then there is *"Perfectionist"* spectator. He is normally accompanied by a few friends. He gleefully points out to his friends every perceived imperfection on your car. Everything he believes that is not "Factory correct", and everything else that doesn't meet his perfectionist values. *"Perfectionist"* spectator rarely talks to *Classic Car Guy* except to say, "That's not original to this car, **IS IT?**" As you are trying to explain that this was an *option* on the car that year, *"Perfectionist"* spectator is already moving on to the next victim/car. After he has finished pointing out imperfections on all of the classic cars, *"Perfectionist"* spectator drives away, with his friends, in his rusted out 1992 mini-van with the caved-in front end.

Then there are the women spectators. Most just walk around and enjoy the beautiful cars and music. However, big cars like my Mercury, and most Cadillac's, Chrysler's, etc. attract the *"Gigglers."* These are normally older women spectators who point to the large back seats in these cars and giggle knowingly. Also these large expensive looking cars attract the *"Hit on the Rich Guy Woman"* spectator. Many women assume that *Classic Car Guy* is rich because he has one of these cars. Comments like "Beautiful car," "Do you live around here," and, "I'd like to ride in this car," are clues. Another clue is that *"Hit on the Rich Guy Women"* do not wear sweet smelling perfumes; they prefer fragrances such as *"New Car"* and *"Burning Rubber."* Oh yes, and leaning way over, looking into your car with their butt up in the air is also a clue.

Hit on the Rich Guy Woman ?

'50s MUSIC AND A DJ to PLAY IT...

'50s, and '60s music is the thing that gives the local car show its sense of being an event. The music combined with the '50s & '60s era cars bring back memories of a different time. Spectators Bip & Bop to the music while enjoying the classic cars. It is a fun time for all. **Then the music stops...** And the voice of the local DJ comes blaring over the speakers. Spectators freeze in the middle of their Bop. *Classic Car Guy* groans. The DJ smiles with self importance. The fun time is shattered...

Before we get to the DJs, let's talk about the music. '50s and '60s music consists equally of soft ballads and loud rock. All local car show DJs have this unique amplifier that instantly recognizes whether the song is a Ballad or Rock. At the first hint of a Ballad the amplifier goes to its lowest volume, and distant sounds like the scanners in the Supermarket across the street drown out the ballads. When the '50s Rock songs come on, the amplifier immediately jacks itself up to about 100 decibels and instantly fries the hearing aids of any *Classic Car Guys* or spectators that are within 500 yards of a speaker. This phenomenon is known in the classic car community as <u>C</u>ompletely <u>R</u>andom <u>A</u>coustic <u>P</u>ulsation (**CRAP**).

Before we discuss the DJs, it is important to note that the DJs are the organizers of the local car shows and without them there would be no local car shows. The thousands of dollars that these car shows earn for charities would not happen except for the DJs. For that we commend them. But that doesn't mean that we're not going to jerk their chains a little.

There are 3 basic types of DJs. The first is "just play the music" guy who just plays music. He only interrupts the music to let you know that the 50/50 raffle has $8 dollars in it. He explains that if you want to buy 50/50 tickets you can get them from Mabel. It is easy to spot Mabel; she is the one in the bright yellow walker with 20 feet of tickets trailing behind her.

Just Play the Music
...and register the cars.

The second type of DJ is the "*Music Buff*", a true music aficionado. He knows every song title and performer since Ralph Waldo Edison first scratched a cylinder. ***Oops, sorry, I meant Tommie Edison, Ralph's brother.*** "*Music Buff*" prefaces each song with a history of the artist and the song. Most of these artists and songs have *unique* histories unknown to the average *Classic Car Guy* and spectator. This is primarily because nobody ever bought their music, except "*Music Buff.*" Next in line is the Trivia music quiz. The "*Music Buff*" asks the *Classic Car Guys* and spectators for the answers to trivia questions about the music he loves. Three *Classic Car Guy Wives* immediately run up to where the *"Music Buff"* is DJ'ing and try to answer all of the trivia questions. Meanwhile all of the *Classic Car Guys* and spectators continue their car show thing, although somewhat subdued due to a lack of music. After the three *Classic Car Guy Wives* go zero for 207 on the trivia questions the music starts again with Gino and the Genoans singing their classic "Offa Da Key" from their album "We Don't Sing So Good."

The final DJ is the *"Entertainer"*, a cross between Rodney Dangerfield and the Reverend Farwell. The *"Entertainer"* has total command of his audience and dominates the microphone with announcements, jokes and verbal

foreplay until he gets hungry. Then the music finally plays, while the *"Entertainer"* dines on the free hot dogs and hamburgers provided by the sponsors. The unique taste of these hot dogs and burgers can, I guess, be attributed to the fact that they are free and you get what you pay for, but the lack of free roaming cats and dogs anywhere near the sponsor's business does make you wonder.

The *"Entertainer"* is at his best with announcements. Simple announcements such as, "Next week's car show will be at Denny's" become 30 minute standup skits. **Please note: next week's show, on the 3rd Sunday of the month, has been at Denny's, on the 3rd Sunday of the month, for the last 27 years.** During these 30 minutes we get to know Denny's owner, his family and how much he loves car shows. We also get to know the *"Entertainer's"* family, *of the last 27 years*, his current weight loss/gain and the date of his next colonoscopy. We also learn in exquisite detail that there will be door prizes, 50/50 drawings and trophies, *just as there has been for the last 27 years*. As a finale to this 30 minute standup event we learn that there will be another announcement right after the first 40 seconds of the next song.

The "Entertainer" is also big on *guest stars* to add to the entertainment of the *Classic car Guys* and spectators. The *guest star* normally appears right before the trophy presentation, making the *Classic Car Guys* a captive audience. The spectators however, are long gone at this point, most likely looking for a car show with some music. So with the *Classic Car Guys* eager for their trophies, the temperature in the low 100s, the humidity in the high 100s and a violent thunderstorm 5 minutes away, "*The Entertainer*" announces a surprise *guest star*. It is "Harvey Milkbutt." Harvey played the second mate on the Gilligan's Island TV show. His character drowned in the opening show and was never actually seen on TV. Harvey is going to tap dance, the entire sound track of West Side Story… And yet, with all this, we still love the "*Entertainer.*"

DOOR PRIZES…

Every car show has door prizes donated by local businesses. Most of the door prizes are items that the local business couldn't sell or wouldn't sell for fear of legal repercussions. Door prize tickets are $1 each, or 51 for $50. The prizes are unique items that *Classic Car Guy* is dying to own, like screwdriver sets. The average *Classic Car Guy* only has between 17 and 23 sets of screwdrivers in his garage. Other unique prizes may be metric allen wrench sets. Although most, if not all, classic cars have no need for metric allen wrenches, winning another set to go with the three sets already in the garage can't hurt, *right?* For this reason most *Classic Car Guys* buy only a few tickets, while *Gotta Win Car*

Guy buys at least 150 tickets. With the exception of one prize, a set of screwdrivers, which go to the lucky *Classic Car Guy* that has only 15 sets in his garage, *Gotta Win Car Guy* takes home all of the door prizes. The fact that *Gotta Win Car Guy* gets all of the door prizes every week and shows up every week in a slightly rusted, in primer car, that he hasn't touched since he bought it 15 years ago, is not lost on *Classic Car Guy*.

"Metric Allen Wrench Set"

I want one!!! I want one!!

As the DJ is calling out the winning door prize ticket numbers, *Classic Car Guy* is doing his thing (sleeping, talking, trying to remember where he is, etc.) and not paying much attention. Consequently, a single number may be called out for up to 10 minutes before the winner realizes he has won. Multiply this by 40 door prizes, add in the temperature (102) and humidity (98) and you have the blood pressure of *Classic Car Guy* waiting for his trophy.

TROPHIES...

There are unwritten rules to bringing a classic car to a local car show. The most important is to memorize the following sentence and to say it aloud and in a heartfelt manner at least 5 times during the show. It is mandatory that this sentence be said immediately before the trophy presentations. It is a short sentence, but it is directly to the point and shows the true essence of *Classic Car Guy*. That sentence is, *"I don't care about trophies."* When said correctly and passionately it can bring tears to the eyes of anyone within hearing distance. If it is said while in a group of other

Classic Car Guys, the following responses from the other *Classic Car Guys* are required: "Me neither." "I got 50 at home." "They just take up space." "Dust collectors."

While it is important to say this sentence aloud, it is equally important to finish the rest of this sentence quietly under your breath. It goes like this *(ALOUD)*, "**I don't care about trophies,**" *(QUIETLY)*, "As long as I win one." Poets may say there is nothing worse than a woman scorned. **Wrong Again, Kemo Baby!!** There is nothing that compares to *Classic Car Guy* not winning a trophy. Wives and children of *Classic Car Guy* can tell by the way he attacks his driveway after a car show, as to whether a trophy was won. With the back door open and car keys in one hand and a note saying, "we're at Mothers" in the other. Wives and their children cautiously watch out the window for his arrival.

At the show, the *Classic Car Guys* that didn't win trophies are models of decorum during the trophy presentations and loudly applaud the winners, while quietly referring to the winning cars as a "Piece of _____": *a short fill in the blank sentence honoring both the winning cars and the judges.* A "Piece of <u>Heaven</u>" being one example, although a rare one! Should *Classic Car Gal* win a trophy the "Piece of _____" tribute may include the word "Nice."

Then there is the guy we like to call the *Trophy Whore*. The *Trophy Whore* will do anything, anytime, anyplace, to get a trophy. The *Trophy Whore* can and will recite, for every trophy he has won, the show name, the date of the show and the reason he deservedly won. The *Trophy Whore* is easy to recognize, as his is the car with trophies on display throughout the car. His trunk is open and filled with trophies; the back seat is filled with trophies; and under the hood lining the engine compartment are his most revered trophies. His trophy display is telling the car guys, the spectators and mostly the judges that he deserves and expects to win a trophy. The judges are well aware of the heated cross examination/temper tantrum that will be coming their way if Trophy Whore doesn't win a trophy. So *Trophy Whore* will most likely win another trophy for his collection. Meanwhile, when *Trophy Whore* is not looking, *Classic Car Guy* is putting his old bowling trophies under *Trophy Whore's* hood. This confuses *Spectator* guy, but Expert Spectator guy does not miss a beat as he explains to his wife that the guy with the bowling ball on top of the trophy is actually the original hood ornament on this make of car.

Speaking of Judges...who decides who gets a trophy? Why the Judges of course!!! And just who are they? Many of the local car shows are sponsored by the establishment that hosts the car show. If Denny's were to sponsor a show and it would be in their parking lot with some of their employees acting as judges. Along with this, a local car club may also be a sponsor and some of their members may be judges. Or the DJ who organized the show will appoint some people to be judges. As you have probably figured out by now, there are no "qualified judges," except by accident, at the local car shows.

It is easy to predict which cars will win trophies at the show as soon as you know who the judges are. If it is one of Denny's female employees then all yellow, red and pink cars will win trophies. If it is a male teenager from Denny's then all bright colored Honda-sized cars will win. If it is an older Denny's employee then all Corvettes will win (it's that "if I won the lottery" thing). If the judge is from a local car club and he owns a classic car, then classic cars will win. If the judge is from a local car club and he owns a street rod, then street rods will win. If the DJ appoints the judges then only those cars that are new to the DJ's show win. **That should bring them back!**

On occasion a car club will hold a show that will be truly judged. Car club members will be instructed in how to judge and will be given a judging sheet which will allow them to rate each car, from 1 – 10, in 5 or more specific areas such as interior, body, engine, etc. So the judges go over every car in detail, individually marking their judging sheets as they inspect each area of the car. Unfortunately, the end result is that 98% of the cars are rated as all 10s. The 2% that were not rated as all 10s happen to be because one judge took *the importance of his position as judge* very seriously, and rated some of the nicest car at the show as 5s or 6s. Why did he do this? *Because he could!!* Meanwhile the other judges are sitting there looking at a stack of judging sheets with all 10s on them. So, after much discussion, they go into "Which one do you like?" mode, and a consensus is reached, and *all of the red cars win*. As there are no women judges, the bright pink Dodge Ram 4x4 Hemi pickup with the 6 foot wheels doesn't get a trophy.

IN SUMMARY...

While I tend to exaggerate the workings of, and people involved in, local car shows, I dare you to say you did not recognize a piece of yourself someplace in this story. I surely spotted myself many times. Please note that I am a *Classic Car Guy* and a local car show guy and it is this hobby that has saved me from a retirement of boredom. So if you want a nostalgic good time, with good music and a great display of automotive art, go to your local car show. Or, better yet, get involved with classic cars. YOU WON'T REGRET IT...

Oh Yea, while you're at your local car show see how many of the people mentioned in this story you can spot. And don't forget to look in the mirror...

Chapter 7
Curse of The Beast

Don't believe in curses? Thought the evil 59 Plymouth from the movie "Christine" was bad? You need to read this...

This is a true story. Names have been changed to protect the guilty. This is what happened and how it happened. There is no end to this story at this time. I don't know how it will end, or when it will end. I can only relate what has happened to date. It's just scary!!!

When I bought my 1969 Mercury Marauder X-100 it was to be a *driver* muscle car. Run around, go to the store, play at the stop lights, etc. When it came out of the body/paint shop it was so perfect it instantly became a show car. Even though it was a show car it was quite fast, but I wanted to go faster. So I sat down with the local speed shop

(Costly Classic Cars) to define what had to be done and what it would cost to make my Marauder go *really* fast. The speed shop's initial cost quote appeared to include enough money for the speed shop owner and his entire staff to retire to the Bahamas in pampered luxury. After much discussion with the owner and his tech staff we were able to define the difference between:

(a) Buying the best, most expensive equipment to set all known world speed records and,

(b) Just going *really* fast.

I was told that the "b" option would cost about $15,000. Teary eyed and shaken I explained that I could not justify putting that much money into what was a show car. Immediately a low pitched wailing sound came from the technician's area of the shop, followed by a high pitched wailing sound from the parts department area. All of this was drowned out by the sound of the speed shop owner tearing up his Bahamas brochures. I quickly departed with a friendly good bye chorus from the speed shop personnel of "Good will and bless", which almost sounded a lot like "God will get you for this."

So I began looking for something else to be my muscle car driver. Everything I looked at was in the $25K - $35K bracket, at a minimum. With every other ad saying, "This is a dang nice car but..." Now, I'm just a Northerner transplanted to Florida 27 years ago. **Florida being a Northern state separated from the North by the South.** Being a Northerner, I don't know what a "dang nice car" is, although I do know they are expensive and there are a lot of them. So between car ads saying: "dang nice car", "95% rust free", "project car", "barn find", and "ya'all ain't gonna believe this", my days were full looking for my driver muscle car.

Since the day I got my Marauder, Bert, a guy I had met through a Marauder Club, had helped me out on my Marauder with advice, parts, etc. He had a black Marauder just like mine, but he had spent the money ($22,000) to make it faster. I kept, kiddingly, asking him when he was going to sell his car to me. A few months ago Bert answered with "How about now?" and gave me a good price; well below what the speed shop wanted to just upgrade my car. I said OK, I would go up to Greensboro, South Carolina and look at Bert's Marauder.

He spent the money HERE. $$$
425 HP

That's when it got weird…

I flew to Atlanta, Georgia to meet Roger who had an auto transport trailer. We hooked up the trailer and began a 6 hour plus journey to Greensboro to see the car, and Bert. Bert had a small engine repair shop on the outskirts of Greensboro. We got to Bert's place and my first thought after 6 hours on the road was, I need a restroom. Bert's shop was a typical repair shop with parts everywhere. Well, Bert had to clear parts and things off the floor in order for me to reach the restroom, which was a door-less, grease covered, lightless room. An adventure all to itself! Actually it brought back memories. Back-in-the-day most of the auto shops I remember were exactly like this.

After we were relieved and escorted out through the

maze of parts from the restroom to the back of the building, we finally saw the car. The car was in much, much better condition than I had imagined. The body and paint were pretty much flawless and the trim, with the exception of the rear bumper needing to be re-chromed, was also flawless. The interior was another story as the dash was a mess and the white driver's seat was closer to black than white. I assume this was from the grease on Bert's mechanic's overalls.

Then Bert started the car. Walls shook, and I could hear windows shattering down the street. Bert explained that he didn't know what kind of mufflers were on the car but they were loud. Roger and I were going, "*What? What? I can't hear you!*"

Bert then said to take it for a ride. I was ready. You could tell this car had some real power just from the sound of the engine. So I pulled out slowly and coasted up to the first stop light. The light is red, and I stop. I look across the intersection and a police car is at the light opposite me. I'm in a car whose mufflers will probably shatter the police car's windshield if I step on it, so when the light turns green I ease forward. The police car goes past and is quickly out of sight and then I stomped on the gas.

You need to understand what "stomped on the gas" means with a Marauder. If I did it with my Marauder (30 mph and kick down to a lower gear) the wheels would squeal and the car would leap forward. My marauder has 360 HP; Bert said his car has in excess of 430 HP so the difference should be significant.

When I stomped on the gas on Bert's 430 HP Marauder--nothing happened--I did it again and *nothing*. I had driven 6 hours to see this car and it isn't anywhere near as powerful as my Marauder. Not a happy camper, I drove back to Bert's shop. (By the way, I found out later that the rod that allows the accelerator to kick the transmission down to a lower gear was disconnected, which is why it appeared to have no power). I told Bert that this car had no power. Bert said, "Let me drive it." I was ready to leave but I agreed, out of courtesy, and got in the car with Bert.

We pulled out of Bert's shop and Bert floored the gas while still in low gear (no kick down required). What happened next took no more than 2 seconds.

The rear wheels screamed--the front-end lifted off the ground--the car did a 180 degree turn--*and tried to eat a stone wall.*

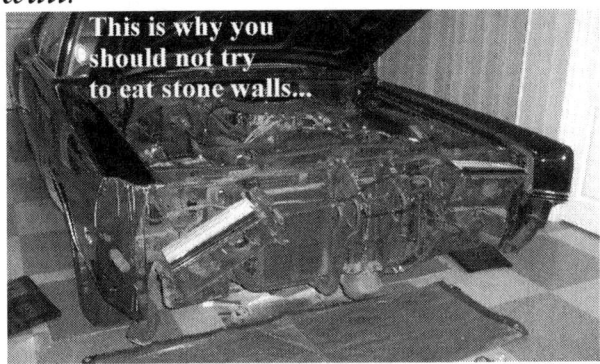

Seconds go by and Bert finally came out of a stupor and said, "It's gotten away from me before but I was always able to recover."

I was numb. *This car is dangerous!* I love it.

Well, the front bumper and part of the grille were bent pretty badly, and Bert offered to take some money off the price. I was uncertain as to what to do. Bert looked at his Marauder and mumbled something about, "Maybe it doesn't want to leave me." *I gave this no thought, although maybe I should have.* I had driven 6 hours to get here and I had another 6 hours more to go back. I was not going home with nothing. So it's a deal. I now own *another black Marauder.*

Then We Started Back...

We loaded up the Marauder for the trip back to Atlanta and then I found out that Roger had decided to take a short cut. He said we will go through Knoxville, Tennessee and get around some of the Atlanta traffic. My only comment was, "Aren't the Smokey Mountains in that direction?" Roger assured me that he had no idea but that it looks flat on the map. We start out and the conversation is pretty much about

The Beast, which is the name we gave the Marauder because of its mighty growl and the fact that it likes to eat stone walls.

We are making pretty good time, with little traffic except a few tractor trailers. As it begins to get dark the road starts uphill, then downhill, then side hill, then more uphill and even more uphill. Tractor trailers by the hundreds appear out of nowhere. They are in front of us, behind us, alongside us, everywhere. Then night falls and it becomes pitch black except for hundreds of tractor trailers, lit up like square Christmas trees. The road becomes a ribbon of lights going up, down and around mountains that we can't see in the night. *We are in the middle of a herd of tractor trailers stampeding through the night.* Their speed is our speed. We're trapped, but Roger keeps his truck on pace with the tractor trailers. The Marauder follows us on its trailer, weaving now and then with each hairpin curve. Hours pass, the stampede continues and Roger drives on with calm assurance. I begin to think that we may live though this after all. **Then the rain starts...**

Three hours later we are still in the mountains. I have a violent headache from the headlights, side lights and Christmas lights of the tractor trailers, not to mention the rain, and am in desperate need of a restroom. Roger is psyched to run non-stop to Atlanta but somehow I convince him to stop. We pull off the interstate looking for somewhere to take a break and: *Uh Oh!!! The dash lights on Roger's truck go out. I hadn't seen this happen in a lot of years, but back-in-the-day the old '50s Fords were famous for electrical problems and dash lights out meant tail lights out also: Uh Oh!!!* We soon find out that 50 years later dash lights out still mean tail lights out, which mean trailer lights out also.

An hour later after going through wiring connections, fuses, etc. with no luck, we decide to make a run for Roger's house by climbing up on the trailer and putting the Marauder's parking lights on to act as our tail lights, and off we go. Two hours later the lights on the Marauder dim. We continue on with tractor trailers flashing and blowing their horns. *Yes, we know we have no tail lights, we know that the lights on the Marauder are dim, yes, we know this is stupid, but...*

The Marauder's lights are almost out but Roger pushes on. We make it to Roger's house in a record 9 ½ hours. It took us 3 ½ hours longer than the ride up to Greensboro, we dueled with tractor trailers, fought the rain, and climbed the Smoky Mountains, *but we missed the Atlanta traffic.* Roger had this look of satisfaction and accomplishment, *rightfully so I guess?* We are completely drained and we decide to leave the Marauder on the trailer overnight. How can so many things go wrong on a simple trip from Greensboro to Atlanta? Bert's parting words of, "Maybe it doesn't want to leave me," pop into my mind. Nah!

Curse of The Beast...

The next day we unload the Beast and put it in Roger's garage/showroom with Rogers's other classic cars.

I need to explain that Rogers garage-- the basement of his large house--was transformed by Roger into a Rolls Royce/Bentley class showroom complete with an exquisitely tiled floor, with walls and ceiling to match. Roger's classic cars are displayed within and the entire area is Roger's protected domain. Were it not for our long friendship I am sure that the Beast would not be welcomed into this pristine setting.

Roger's Showroom

I am flying back to Bradenton but the Beast will stay here with Roger. The game plan from the beginning was for the car to stay at Rogers a few months until Roger's schedule allowed him to make a trip to Bradenton so we could do a little fishing, with the Beast following behind on his trailer. The Beast's bite out of the stone wall changed that scenario a bit, as now Roger will try to repair the front end before heading to Bradenton. The challenge now was to find/repair parts for the Beast. As Roger drove me to the airport, he explained his game plan. He would tear down the front end and determine the damage. If a part was reasonably repairable he would get that done. If it was beyond repair then I would search the world of classic car parts to find the part, if possible.

After Roger dropped me off at the airport he returned home to find his garage/showroom reeking of gasoline. The Beast had sprung a leak in a gas line and Roger's exquisite tile floor was covered with gas. I am convinced that my friendship with Roger was the only thing that kept the Beast from being burned at the stake that day. Looking back, I am sure that Roger now rues his decision to allow the Beast to live.

This was the first of many incidents that caused Roger to believe that the Beast was cursed. He quoted Bert's last words, "Maybe it doesn't want to leave me," and the movie Christine, where the evil 1959 Plymouth wreaked havoc. He made a very strong case for the Beast being cursed. Every time he did something to the Beast it would cause something to go bad for Roger. Dumping gas on the floor was only the first in a long line of incidents. A sample of which is below:

Roger: Take front bumper to shop get fixed.

Beast: Rock breaks Roger's truck's windshield returning from the shop.

Roger: Remove all damaged parts from the front end.

Beast: Truck transmission goes bad.

For the next 2 months every time Roger worked on the Beast something bad would happen immediately after. This

included:
- Stone hitting windshield of truck.
- Truck transmission going bad.
- Truck Water pump going bad.
- Truck intake manifold gasket blowing.
- Golf cart batteries going dead after checking out good the day before.
- Lawn tractor battery goes dead.
- Farm-All Cub tractor refused to start for two days.
- Bumper returned from the shop was the wrong one.
- Nose piece (critical part) damaged in shipment.

Roger called me and asked if it was alright to come to my place for a fishing trip a month earlier than originally planned. This was fine by me. I didn't ask Roger why he was coming a month early. My guess would be that he was trying to get rid of the "cursed" Beast, hoping that delivering it to its rightful owner might eliminate the curse.

Roger's trip from Atlanta to Bradenton was uneventful and the Beast was put into my garage without incident. Roger walked me through what he had done with the Beast and what remained to be done. The rest of the week was fishing and visiting. The Beast remained in the garage, out of sight and out of mind. When it was time for Roger to leave he turned very serious and told me to be careful as, "The Beast is cursed." I laughed it off. Roger was not amused. So I said, seriously, that I would be careful, and he wished me well and headed back to Atlanta.

It was a few uneventful days before I could get to do anything with the Beast. As it happened, my son Mike and his friend Louis stopped by. Mike asked about the car and I offered to take both of them for a ride. Loud mufflers and all, we did a little rampaging through the neighborhood. The boys were impressed with the Beast's power and Louis loved the loud mufflers. After our ride I pulled the Beast into the garage, first letting the boys out because of the close quarters. Once in the garage I do what we all seem to do with powerful cars, I put the shift into park and revved the engine before shutting it down.   But the Beast jumped out of *Park* into *Reverse* when I revved it.   Meanwhile Louis was kneeling down behind the Beast trying to get a good look at the mufflers. Luckily the floors of the garage were epoxy coated and slick enough that the Beast's rear tires screamed and spun out and didn't leap backward into Louis. I was able to brake and go back into *Park* before the Beast moved back at all. The scream from the tires had Louis tumbling backward and sideways to get away from the Beast. Louis asked if I did that on purpose, and I apologized and tried to explain what happened.

When the boys left, I turned and looked at the Beast, and two sets of burnt black rubber marks stared up at me from the garage floor.

The Curse Hits the Fan...

The Beast is now mine and it needs some work to become a daily driver and even more work to maybe become a show car, of sorts. First priority is to be a reliable daily driver. So I put new plugs in it, change the air filter, adjust the carburetor, set the timing, and--it runs like crap. Starting and normal speed is not a problem but when I punch the gas to the floor it spits and sputters like an animal that doesn't want to be tamed. I adjust and test drive, and adjust and test drive some more. Finally I find a loose connection on the automatic choke. Once fixed, the Beast seems to settle down. It's time for a test drive. The Beast roars out from my driveway, rubber burning, and we are off down the road through my test track, which is a quiet adjoining neighborhood. As we reach the furthest point from my house the Beast spits, sputters and coughs and then it stops. *Won't start*--I start adjusting--*Won't start*--I curse and scream--*Won't start!!!*

Finally I call my neighbor Bill, a retired Ford mechanic with a lot of experience on 429 engines like the Beast's, and he adjusts--*Won't start*--Bill adjusts some more--*Won't start!!!* Lastly I call the tow truck and we get the Beast towed back to my house.

Bill and I work on the Beast for 2 days. *Won't start*--Bill is beyond himself. He said it had to start--*Won't start!!!*

Again I call the tow truck and have it towed to the local speed shop. I explain the problem, outline what Bill and I have done, and ask the speed shop tech what he thinks. He said let's see what happens when I try to start it. He turns the key--**AND IT STARTS!** And it just sits there and purrs contentedly. I look at the Beast in disbelief. It looks back at me and smiles evilly--*At least I think it did???*

I tell the speed shop to tune it and adjust whatever is necessary to make it start and run like a real car. Money is no object I tell him. Two days later I return to the speed shop to pick up the Beast. I find that the speed shop took me at my word that "money is no object" and three credit card limits later the bill is paid. I leave the speed shop and the Beast is running well. I stomp on it and WHOA!! It's running really well. Relieved I pull the Beast into its garage. Put it in *Park* and race that beautiful powerful engine--**and it jumps into reverse**. Wheels scream, rubber burns and I hold the brake down for all I am worth. When my heartbeat finally returns to normal I get out of the car, walk to the back, and a new set of burnt black rubber marks stare up at me. Had the Beast marked its territory? **No!! No!! No!!**

This brings about a long

The Beast marks its territory???

evening with Jack and Jim (Daniels and Beam), which eventually evolves into a following morning hangover. Bert's words of, "Maybe it doesn't want to leave me," and Roger's reference to "Christine" and to the Beast being cursed beat against my skull. *It can't be!! No such thing!!* I decide to let the Beast rest for awhile. I need to rest for awhile. So I lock the garage and go fishing for two days. *Fishing* being the correct word; *catching* not being the correct word, as I caught nothing. *Can the Beast influence fishing? I know what Roger's answer would be...*

A few days later I decide to take the Beast out for a run. It starts easily, the engine purrs with a throaty rumble. I gun it a bit and it roars approvingly. Life is good. The Beast and I head out of the driveway. Traffic is somewhat heavy as the local school had just let out. I ease the Beast into traffic and it purrs right along. Two blocks down the road traffic picks up speed and the Beast joins in, with the purring becoming more of a steady roar. We are cruising along, *this is cool*, and then... **The Hood Pops Open!!!** *It's black in front of me!!! I can't see past the hood!!!* I slow down and try to get off the road, but I can't see the road shoulder. *Note: As Florida is basically a swamp that had been drained to allow homes to be built, the road shoulders in Florida are large drainage ditches and going off the road can be a disaster.*

I finally slow to a stop, *in traffic*. Horns are blowing behind me. I get out and close the hood and pull off the road, carefully. I survey the damage: the hood looks OK except for the edges near the windshield which are turned up at a 90 degree angle and look like the wing tips on a manta ray. The hood appears to latch correctly and I head back to the house. Looks like a long night with Jack and Jim.

It takes 2 weeks to get a body shop appointment and another week in the body shop before the hood is fixed. I finally go to pick up the Beast and it is looking really good. The body shop was supposed to be good, and I guess they are- -and I am impressed. The bill for the body work on the hood is 4 pages long. *It's a big hood but... Just checking, I take a quick look around for Bahamas brochures.* I max out more credit cards, and holding back tears I get in the Beast and head for home. I make a right turn out of the body shop, go one block and make another right turn on to the main drag and... **BANG!!!** A pickup truck comes out of a driveway and smashes into the Beast. I cry out *"No, No"* and fall over the steering wheel in shock. *No!! No!! No!! I... just...got...it...fixed...*

I finally sit up and look over at the pickup truck and... 27 Mexicans are piling out of the pickup and running toward me. I leap out of the Beast in **panic!!** I throw my hands up in the air and *scream*. **No Habla Illegal!! No Habla Illegal!!**

As the Mexicans surround me, I fall to my knees and... the pickup truck driver apologies to me in perfect English and hands me his insurance card. The 27 Mexicans morph into just the driver and a passenger. Panic subsides, and with the Beast purring contentedly, *and I think smiling*, we all head back to the Body shop...

A week later the body shop calls, saying the Beast is ready. I pick up the Beast and the body work looks great. COOL!! I start for home, only 5 miles, taking the back roads and keeping an eye out for pickup truck gangs and the Mexican army. The Beast purrs and I arrive home without incident. Whew!!! Had the Curse run its course? Had the Beast fulfilled its vengeance toward me? I dust the Beast off and put on the dust cover, nothing but the best for the Beast. I lock the garage and head for the house.

As I get to the house I see the Costly Air truck parked in my driveway. I go inside, and it's hot. The Costly Air guy said that the A/C Heat pump had died. A little over $10,000 should get a new one. In the distance, in the direction of the garage I hear muted laughter. *No, can't be...*

A week of 95 degrees and 95% humidity later my new A/C unit arrives. Six hours to install and it finally powers up. Four hours later, the house still isn't cool. The A/C unit screams along but can't cool the house. *Not a problem*, Costly Air guy said. Six weeks and 8 different Costly Air technicians later the Factory Rep finally shows up. He takes one look and said the A/C cover (horizontal flow) is the wrong one; a vertical flow cover will fix the problem. *We're saved!* Factory rep makes a phone call and informs me that they are on back order (2 weeks). *Okay, who's laughing?? I can hear you!!* Factory Rep and Costly Air guy look at me strangely.

Two weeks later, after a 10 minute installation of the vertical flow cover, the house cools off. Life is good. The A/C is turned down to 60 degrees and I have a sweater on, life is really good.

Two days later as I go out to my combination office/mother-in-law apartment. I open the door, *and it's hot.* The A/C unit for my office had stopped. A quick call to Costly Air and I am told by the Costly Air service technician that just installed my house A/C unit, that he thought the office unit was on its last legs. He was sure that $7,000 would be enough for a new unit. *Who's that laughing out there??* The new unit was installed without incident. Cool was the order of the day throughout the household. Then the septic system backed up ($1,500), my nephew (on my wife's side) blew up the motor on my boat ($7, 500) and I got this red rash all over my body...

THAT'S IT!!! THE BEAST HAS TO GO...

Dash is a MESS!!!

I make up a For Sale sign and head out to a local car show. No one is interested. The dash is a mess and the interior is just as bad. I can't give it away... I start back toward home and the

Beast's A/C unit goes out. Ten very hot miles later I'm home. I call Costly Classic Cars and am told that $1,500 - $2,000 should fix it. With the A/C fixed and blowing cold I head for the next car show. Again, no interest.. I head for home and the Beast just stops, in traffic, horns blowing, everything is dead. Cars are flying by me in the two adjacent lanes and I can't get out of the car to open the hood. Finally a cop shows up and pushes me to the side of the road. I open the hood and everything electrical is dead.

Luckily, Costly Classic Cars shop is less than a mile away. I call, and they immediately dispatch their top technician out to help me, Two hours later, he shows up. He announces that the alternator is dead. He puts a fully charged battery under my hood and directs me back to his shop. Two weeks later the alternator, voltage regulator and every other electrical what-ever-ator is replaced. *Bank loans are getting harder to get...*

No more trips to car shows to sell the Beast. I put the Beast on eBay with pictures. But unfortunately the pictures include the messed up interior. I'm trying to be honest about the car. The bidding goes up to about the cost of 2 months worth of gas for the Beast! Honest doesn't work; actually honest sucks. So back into the restoration shop and 6 weeks and $4,500 later the Beast is looking good. The dash sparkles, the interior invites-- and my other septic system goes out ($1,400). *Noooo!!!* Back on eBay, the Beast, looking good, sells for top dollar. I am

The Beast is looking GOOD!!!

in shock. Will the new buyer actually pay me and take the car, before a meteor hits my house?

The new buyer arrives, not a pleasant sort, must be that New York attitude. He goes over the Beast with magnets and other stuff. When he is finished he asks to drive the car. I was prepared for this. The Beast is not moving until I have the money and he has the car. If the Beast moves it could destroy itself, the driver, myself, the West Coast of Florida, etc. I politely tell the new buyer that he can't drive it, as I have cancelled the insurance on it. Not a happy camper, he starts the Beast and puts it in all of its gears. Nothing bad happens? No shrapnel flying? No gears breaking? Nothing? Has the Beast found its match?

The new buyer pays me and drives off with the Beast. I am paranoid, what will the Beast do to the new owner, will he survive?? Three days later I get an email from the new owner. I am afraid to open it... I break out in a sweat. Open a beer. Take a deep breath, and open the email. The new owner wants to know what kind of wax I use on the Beast and where does he go for parts. It is running great and he loves it. I respond with a seven page email giving him everything I know about the Beast and where to go for what. He should never have to contact me again, I hope. I debate, with myself, whether I should subscribe to a New York newspaper so I can monitor the bankruptcy and obituary sections.

Nope, I'm not going to do that. It's over. The Beast is gone--Life is good now.

Oops, spilled my beer on the keyboard. ***Noooo!!!***

Chapter 8
And the Curse is Gone?
I learn to hate animals and James Dean...

Part One – Broncos and Pit Bulls...

The Beast has been sold and, hopefully, the curse has gone with it. I have cash burning a hole in my pocket from the sale and I am wildly scanning all of the classic car web sites looking for my next car. Wow, too many cars, and I like almost all of them. How do I make a choice? Then in a brilliant move--I decide to look for cars close to where I live so there are no shipping charges. So I search the classic car web sites based on my zip code, and I find a 1972 Ford Bronco just a few miles away. It is priced at $1,500 which sounds really cheap. The ad says it needs some work but it has a recently installed Ford 302 engine and a three speed transmission on the floor.

It's time for some research to check the current market for Broncos. So I go out to some of the major classic car web sites looking at Broncos. Wow, they are selling for $15,000 - $20,000 and up. This sounds like an investment to me. But I better have this Bronco checked out, so I call Earl at Costly Classic Cars and promise to buy him dinner if he will go with me to check out the Bronco. Earl agrees to check it out in exchange for dinner, as long as he picks which restaurant. I really don't want to go to Billy Bob's Tattoo Parlor & Rib Shack, but what the hell, one meal won't kill me. I make a call to get directions to the Bronco and the following day Earl and I head over to see it. We find the place pretty easily. It's on the outskirts of town in an area where most of the really nicer homes are the single wide trailers in mobile home parks.

We find the address and pull into the yard and there it is, and it's not looking so good. We go to get out of my truck and are immediately surrounded by four large pit bulls that appear to be in very nasty moods. Finally someone comes out of the house and calls off the pit bulls *(But they don't seem to be too happy about it).* Maynard introduces himself and we walk over to see the Bronco. While it didn't look so good from a distance, it looks *so much worse* up close. I am ready to get out of here but Earl asks Maynard to start up the Bronco. Maynard jumps in and turns the key and it starts right up. Of course there are no mufflers on it, and the roar gets the pit bulls into somewhat of a frenzy and they are barking louder than the

Not looking so good...

exhaust on the Bronco, and moving closer to me. They aren't looking very happy. *(I hate it when pit bulls don't look happy.)*

Well the engine sounds good, no smoke out of the exhaust and it rumbles steadily at idle. We ask Maynard to shut it down and we look over the rest of the car. Nothing on the car is in good condition, interior--exterior--nothing!!! The driver's door is caved in and the window smashed, but Maynard shows us a new/used door that he bought. The door is still in the shipping crate and looks pretty good.

I pull Earl aside and ask him what he thinks. He says "it's a good deal." I say "Huh!" Earl explains that for about $10,000 he can fix it up and then I would have a $20,000 plus Bronco. Well Earl is the expert (and also the guy who will get $10,000 to fix it) so I say okay. We settle on $1,300 with Maynard and close the deal.

Two days later the tow truck arrives with the Bronco and unloads it next to my upfront garage where I keep the Marauder. The next day I go to see Earl, at Costly Classic Cars, and to ask him when he can start work on the Bronco. Earl hems and haws and finally says that he has a lot of work right now and it would be six to nine months before he could start work on the Bronco. I'm floored, and ask Earl why he didn't tell me this before. Earl answers, in perfectly logical redneck-ese, "You didn't ask me." I try to explain that I bought this to be a *driver* while it was being restored and not to have it sit for 6-9 months. None of this seems to faze Earl, so I quickly look around for a loose tire iron, and I... I... I..., take the high road instead, and head for home (*Do you hear someone laughing?*). Heading for home I decide that if I have to wait that long to get the Bronco worked on, then I need to put it on the concrete pad alongside my house and cover it with a tarp to keep it out of the Florida weather. I had already put the new/used Bronco door on the pad after removing it from the packing case. So I jump in the Bronco and turn the key, and it starts right up. Cool...

Please Note: It is slightly downhill, from where the Bronco was parked, to the concrete parking pad alongside my house where I am going to store it. Also at the end of this concrete pad there is a two foot drop off down to a concrete driveway, which I use to get my tractor into the house-side garage. Beyond this drop off and driveway there is a steep incline of some 30 feet down to the river. Keep this in mind, it is important...

I put the Bronco into reverse and slowly back it up so it is pointed toward the house. I go to put it into first gear and it doesn't seem to want to go in. Finally I am able to get it in third gear and, easing the clutch out, I start toward the house. I am half way down to the house when I start to brake to slow it down a bit and... *no brakes.* I push hard on the brake pedal... *no brakes.* I am pushing and stomping with all I have--*and no brakes--and we are rolling.* So I grab the emergency brake pull hard, and it comes off the floor in my hand--*and we are rolling.* So I turn off the engine and we start to slow down, but we are in downhill mode--*and we are rolling.* So I go to shift into reverse to try to stop it, hopefully without blowing the transmission. I get it out of third gear but it won't go into reverse, if fact it won't go into any gear now, it's stuck in neutral--*and we are rolling.* I look for something to run into or brush up against that might stop me, but the only thing between me, the drop off and the river is my new/used Bronco door which is lying on the side of the pad. I am hoping that it might be enough to slow me down and keep me from going over the concrete drop off and down the hill into the river. I steer toward the new/used door and catch it with the right front wheel, with the sound of shattering glass in my ear the Bronco slows down...then I catch the right rear wheel on the new/used door and the Bronco slows some more... just before it rolls over the door and heads toward the drop off.

Then the front wheels hit the edge of the drop off and down we go. As the wheels go over the drop off, the frame of the Bronco hits the edge of the concrete. Steel scrapes concrete for what seems to be hours and the Bronco slowly comes to a stop, teetering on the edge of the drop off. Instantly I am out of the Bronco and franticly putting blocks under the back wheels so it doesn't go forward anymore. If had gone another two feet the back wheels would have cleared the drop off and the Bronco and I would be swimming in the Braden River... *Is that laughter I hear???* Fifteen minutes later the Bronco is up on Craig's List and a week later it sells, at a loss, and is towed away. An hour after the tow truck leaves with the Bronco, Earl calls and says that he has an opening and he can start on the Bronco right now. I hang up on Earl and immediately call my wife's cousin Guido in New Jersey and give him the address of Costly Classic Cars... Er... actually I didn't do that; I just sat down and had a very long conversation with Jack (Daniels). I am beginning to warm to Jack's philosophy about life, as Jack puts it "Life sucks and then you die..." Jack is not an optimist!!!

...and we are rolling!

Fool me once, shame on you--fool me twice, shame on me--fool me three times--er--more about that later...

With the Beast coming close to killing me financially and the Bronco almost killing me (drowning) for real, I have learned my lesson. I don't need another car. I have the Widow, my Mercury Marauder X-100, a rare pristine show car, I don't need anything else. *Hooray for me!!!* No more surfing the internet looking for cars to buy. I have the Widow and money in my pocket, life is good....

Of course as a Mercury Marauder owner, I am forced to search the internet looking for other Mercury's like my Marauder to keep track of the market out there. Some three months after the Bronco incident, I am surfing the web looking at Mercury's and, *holy crap*, there is a 49 Mercury coupe for sale and it is only 50 miles from me. The asking price is $15,000 and this is potentially a $50 - $60 thousand dollar car. *Sounds like an investment to me!!!* Actually I didn't see it as an investment. Instead, in my mind, I saw James Dean in the movie *Rebel Without a Cause*. This is James Dean's car--I could be James Dean if I owned the car.

Who is James Dean? Good question! People my age know exactly who James Dean is, and when they see a '49-'50 Mercury they know it is James Dean's car. The younger generation when they see a '49-50 say "That's Sylvester Stalone's car from the movie Cobra." Since it's my book, we are staying with James Dean.

James Dean was an actor and a teen age idol, for guys as well as girls. The Movie "Rebel Without a Cause" was James Dean's first movie. It was one of the first rebellious teenage movies ever made. It was a massive hit and James Dean became one of Hollywood's biggest stars based on this movie. In the movie he wore a red nylon windbreaker, with the collar up, and drove 1949 Mercury. He was the definition of COOL!!! If you were a guy, and you lived in that era you owned a red nylon windbreaker and wore it with the collar up, and would have killed to own a 1949 Mercury.

Okay, I know that this is stupid. I don't need this car, and I don't even want this car, but it wouldn't hurt to look at it, *would it?* Now 50 miles is a long trip to just go look at a car by myself. I should probably find someone to go with me, share the ride, ease the boredom of the ride, etc. Also it wouldn't hurt if the person was a car expert, someone honest with only my interests in mind. *Well, good luck finding that guy...* So I called Earl.

Immediately that voice deep in the back of my head calls out to me asking, "What was that *'Fool me three times'* thing again?"

Part Two – I am not James Dean

This time it takes both a lunch and a dinner to convince Earl to go with me to see the '49 Merc. Billy Bob's Tattoo Parlor & Rib Shack--two meals-- in the same day--that's going to hurt. So late on Saturday morning Earl and I head north on I-75 toward Tampa. As we pass each small town on the way Earl relates his past adventures in each, making the miles go by ever so slowly. Finally we arrive at a nice older neighborhood on the outskirts of Tampa and the '49 is sitting in the driveway, all in primer, but looking pretty good.

I stop my truck in the driveway next to the '49. *Out of nowhere, '50s music floods my brain, "I'm a rebel and I...",* and then the door to the house opens and James Dean steps out and walks toward the truck. I jump out of the truck and rush to meet James Dean, who immediately morphs into a 12 year old kid with his Momma right behind him. Momma introduces herself and Harold, the 12 year old, who is actually 18 years old (yeah right!!!).

Harold, in a squeaky voice, begins to tell us about the

49. It has a Chevy 350 engine and a Chevy 700R4 transmission, both completely rebuilt. Harold gives us a sheet of paper listing the components that constituted the rebuild of the 350 engine. Earl and I look it over, and *wow*, if there were any aftermarket parts you wanted to put into a Chevy 350 to make it one awesome butt kicking engine, these were the parts. Earl and I are both impressed. I ask Harold, which of the major hotrod shops in Tampa did the rebuild on the 350.

Beaming, Harold replies squeakily, "I did it myself."

I'm thinking *"Okay, I'm out of here"*, but before I can say anything Earl asks Harold to start up the '49. The words "déjà vu" and "Bronco" nibble at my brain, but then the 49 starts up and it sounds really good. The engine purrs and a pair of "cherry bomb" mufflers crackle with each rev of the engine. Immediately James Dean reappears, and he smiles at me. James Dean never smiles; *this must be a really good car*. All of this is interrupted by Earl telling Harold that we need to take the car for a ride.

Harold then begins a lengthy story about the '49. It seems that he was working on the car in conjunction with a hotrod shop in Tampa. The car had been stripped down to be painted in primer and every latch and handle, door, hood, trunk, etc., was removed in preparation. It was at this point, right after being primered that the hotrod shop went out of business and the owner took off for parts unknown; along with all known parts of the '49. Luckily the '49 was left behind, looking fresh in its new coat of primer, but without any latches or handles of any kind.

Ah ha!!! This explained the vast amount of bungee cords throughout the car. The doors and trunk were held down with bungee cords but the hood was not. So Harold suggested that we should not go very fast in our test drive. We didn't, as at about 15 miles per hour the hood would begin to rise up. After a slow ride I ask Earl what he thinks about the car. Earl says it's a great deal. I say, "Huh!!!" *(Does any of this sound familiar?)* Earl explains that from what he can see, $20,000 should cover it and this can easily be a $50,000 car. Let me calculate this out; *Déjà vu + Bronco x 2 = Fool me three times.* Not going to happen. Not going to give Earl $20,000, which I don't have any way. As I turn away and start for the truck, *James Dean suddenly appears--he is smiling--he is taking off his red nylon windbreaker--with the collar still up on it--and-- and-- he is handing it to me.*

So Harold agrees to take $11,500 for the '49 and I am the new owner and Earl and I head back to Bradenton. This time Earl does not talk about his past adventures and the trip goes fast with Earl busy on his cell phone talking to various Chevy dealers about buying a new Camaro.

I get home and immediately go online looking for latches and handles for the '49. There are none on eBay. Uh Oh!! Finally I find the Old Mercury Car Stuff web site and all of the latches and handles I need are there. I am saved! Then I look at the prices for each and realize that these must be the gold plated ones. I soon realize that any part for a '49 Merc, while not gold plated, is priced as if it were solid gold. I call Earl and scream out, "Did you know parts were that expensive for a '49 Mercury?"

Earl replies, "Yep" and suggests to me that I need to ask questions if I want to know things like that. Earl then says to me, "I'm sure you know that the $20,000 is just for parts. The labor is extra and, oh yeah, the rate for labor just went up to $95 an hour. " Then in a more sincere tone of voice, Earl kindly says, "But since we're friends, I'll give you a deal on the labor costs--$85 for you."

Throw money in the window...

I am now officially in panic mode. I am thinking where the hell am I going to get $20,000 plus labor costs, and do they even make red nylon windbreakers any more. I look around for James Dean for help; he is nowhere to be found. Earl Interrupts my thinking and says he has to go test drive a new Camaro and hangs up on me. As I look around for Jack (Daniels) my wife comes in and says that the transmission in her car just went out, and that we need a new kitchen…

(Does anybody out there think that this is going to go well for me???)

A year goes by and I continue my weekly visits to see the '49 at Costly Classic Cars. As I do each week, I roll down the window on the car and throw money inside. Earl's new Camaro is looking really nice and he tells me he is considering buying another one for his wife. I am hard pressed to keep from asking Guido to "talk" to Earl, but I don't. If I did call Guido, I would send him after James Dean instead. After all, *it was all his fault.*

I guess if I learned anything from this, it is (a) that you cannot buy a red nylon windbreaker anywhere, and (b) that **"I am not James Dean…"**

Chapter 9
Hilton Head Island Concours d' Elegance

Going big time--with more than a few bumps along the way...

Roger and I finished the restoration of my Marauder in November of 2003. After a few ACCA shows, in which I won a few trophies, and spending weekends at local car shows, I was really into car shows. Then I heard about the Devereaux-Kaiser Car Show in Sarasota, Florida. This is the largest car show on the West Coast of Florida, and is held on the last Sunday in January each year. It normally attracts about 1,200 plus cars from all over the Southeast. To a new classic car guy like me, this show sounded really cool. So in January of 2005 I took my Marauder to the Devereaux-Kaiser show.

1,200 cars!!! There had to be at least that many. Classic cars as far as you can see. So I began what became a day long ritual, of going out and looking at a few hundred cars and then returning to my car for a while and then repeating this over and over. At one point during the show when I returned from one of my ritual tours of looking at cars I found a card on my Marauder's windshield. It had a Hilton Head Island logo and a name and cell phone number on it. Scribbled on it was a hand written note asking me to call the cell number. I did, and a gentleman answered and said he would come over to my car to see me. He did, and he introduced himself and said he was a scout for the Hilton Head Island Concours d' Elegance and wanted to know if I would be interested in taking my car to Hilton Head Island, South Carolina for the Concours. I immediately answered, "Huh!!!" He then proceeded to explain to me that a Concours d' Elegance was the top of the line when it came to car shows and that Hilton Head was among the top four in the country. The Hilton Head Concours was by invitation only and would be limited to 100-150 cars and he wanted my Marauder to be one of these cars.

Somewhat in awe and a bit dumbfounded I said, "Are you sure you want my Marauder?" He said "Yes" and so I said "Okay." He gave me an application to fill out and submit to the Concours Committee for their acceptance along with photos of my car. I asked what if they rejected my application. He said not to worry as he will be sponsoring my acceptance. I did as he said and my car was accepted.

Over the next months I got everything organized for this great event in my very young classic car career. My brother-in-law and his family were joining my wife and me at Hilton Head for the weekend. Other family members were trying to make arrangements also. It was almost becoming a family reunion. The most critical item in the preparation process was getting a covered trailer to transport what would be a fully detailed, looking good Marauder to Hilton Head. My *friend* Earl had a covered trailer and said he would transport the car, stay for the Concours, and then trailer it back. Everything was now a *"GO."* That is until a few days before the Concours, when I called my "friend" Earl to check that all was okay, and he told me that he had just traded his trailer for a pair of four wheelers and was on his way to the mountains with them.   *Uh Oh!!!*   I asked, "What about transporting my car to Hilton Head?"

He said, "They are really nice four wheelers."

I calmly told my friend how happy I was for him while scanning the Yellow Pages for the heading "Hit Men."

Too late to recover, although I tried, I called the people at Hilton Head and apologized profusely. They were very sympathetic and understanding and told me not to worry and they invited me to come to the Concours the following year. They even sent me the brochure for this year's Concours with a picture of my car in it and a license plate for my car with the Hilton Head Concours d' Elegance logo and my name on it. It was very classy and very nice of them.

For the next few years I had "sort of" an open invitation to the Hilton Head Concours. Complications, medical and financial, caused me to miss these Concours'. Finally in September of 2009, I added the Concours d' Elegance at Hilton Head Island to what was now my "Bucket List" and called Hilton Head and asked if I could still get into this year's Concours (November 2, 2009). This was on a very short notice, to say the least.

Again the people at Hilton head couldn't have been nicer. They explained that my cars class was full but they had an opening in the Performance Class which was featuring "pony cars" this year. While I didn't exactly fit in that class my Marauder would be a great example of a full size muscle car in comparison to the pony cars. Also because I didn't fit in the class, they felt that it would not be fair to judge my Marauder against the pony cars and that my car would have to be "Display Only" and not be judged. Not a problem, I said yes immediately. *Cross one off the Bucket List.*

Based on past history, my major concern now was getting transport for my Marauder to Hilton Head. The standard industry transport company pricing structure would require me to take a second mortgage on my house to pay for the transport to Hilton Head. They also would not give me a specific pickup, or return date and time, which was a logistics problem for me as I had to coordinate my departure and arrival (air and driving) with the departure (loading) and arrival (unloading) of the Marauder. So I looked for transport locally. I tried friends, friends of friends, car clubs, etc. with no luck. Then in a stroke of genius, I called a local classic car dealer and asked if he had people that transported the cars he bought and sold. The dealer said, "Call Paulo". So I did, and Paulo said, "Sure, not a problem." Paulo sounded like a good guy but I told him I wanted to check out his trailer before we made the deal for transport.

So I took the Marauder over to Paulo's place and we measured it against the size of the trailer. We had two inches to spare on each side at the tires and about six inches each side at the body. Close fit all the way around! It looked like I would have to lose 20 lbs. to squeeze through the car door, which would barely open, to get out of the car once I had driven it on the trailer. Paulo said not to worry. So

Checking out Paulo's trailer

the deal was made. Paulo and his brother would trailer the car out to Hilton Head on Friday evening. They would stay in Hilton Head over the weekend and play golf, so they would be there for the return transport of the car. I wanted the car transported to Hilton Head on Friday so if there was a problem during the transport there was time on Saturday to recover and still make it to Hilton Head for the Concours on Sunday. I would, on my own, meet up with Roger and his wife, Leann, in Atlanta on Friday and we would drive to Hilton Head to meet up with Paulo and my car. This was perfect, what could go wrong?

Paulo was scheduled to pick up the Marauder on Thursday for the Friday trip to Hilton Head Island. I called Paulo on Thursday morning to set a time for the pickup. "There is a change of plans," Paulo says. He explained that his brother was sick so he didn't have anyone to golf with. So he would take the Marauder up on Saturday evening. I explained to Paulo that this was too late, that there were no "do over's" on this trip. If there was a problem during the transport and the Marauder wasn't in Hilton Head, ready for the Concours, at 7:00 a.m. on Sunday everything was lost: the Concours, the weekend, expenses, etc. Paulo insisted that there wouldn't be any problems and he would make it on time if he left on Saturday.

I was in a state of panic and screamed at Paulo, "If you don't make it to Hilton head on time I'll take the money you should be getting for the transport and hire a hit man."

Paulo said back, "If I don't make it on time I'll give you the name and number of a hit man." We finally settled on Paulo leaving very early Saturday morning so he would be in Hilton Head by 8:00 a.m. Saturday so Roger and I could check out the car and do any last minute detailing in preparation for Sunday. *Saturday morning came* --I took a deep breath--and we went look for Paulo. We finally found Paulo, and my Marauder, in the farthest end of transport parking area waiting for us. *I exhaled...*

From this point forward everything went great. We spent Saturday at Hilton Head's Motoring Festival which was on the grounds of Honey Horn Plantation. This consisted of 2 parts. Part 1 was an area of upscale automobile vendors showing off their top of the line cars and offering drives in these cars. "Want to drive this Mercedes 560 SL roadster by AMG?"

"Sure!!!"

"Here are the keys, go for it." Jaguar, Porsche, Infinity, etc. were all there offering drives. No selling was allowed, just information and drives. *Very cool!* Interspersed with the automobile vendors were large displays of vintage motorcycles, military vehicles, motor homes, boats, cars, etc, etc. *Absolutely awesome!* Many, if not most, of the vehicles were ones I had never seen before. Others brought back great memories of back-in-the-day. Just this alone was worth the trip.

Also in this area was the registration station for the Concours. I went to sign up the Marauder, gave them my name, and in seconds it was like I was a long lost family member. They welcomed me and they seemed to know about my Marauder and said they were anxious to see it. The Concours staff was gracious, hospitable, friendly and very professional in what they were doing, but mostly they just seemed like nice people having fun doing their job. I had some thoughts prior to arriving here that the Concours event might be a stiff and uppity affair. So far, nothing could be further from the truth. This is going to be *FUN!!!*

Part 2 was a very large car show put on by a number of large car clubs. It was just across a small access road in that part of Honey Horn Plantation that the Concours d' Elegance would be held on Sunday. There were cars that I hadn't seen since back-in-the-day, some cars that I didn't remember and a lot of cars that I was familiar with from the many car shows I have been to. But what hit me the most was the quality of the cars. *Outstanding cars!* My thoughts were: *If this is what the car show cars look like, what will the Concours cars look like?* I guess, just then, I got a little nervous about my Marauder being in the Concours, but Roger settled me down and we decided we were here to have fun and show people what a Mercury Marauder X-100 was all about.

Sunday morning finally came and at 7:00 a.m. we met Paulo at the transport parking lot and unloaded the Marauder. It was a very short drive to Honey Horn and the Concours grounds, less than 3/4 of a mile. We were greeted warmly and directed to our Class display area. They parked us and put up a display board in front of the car with details of my Marauder on it and also hung a license plate below it with the Hilton Head Island Concours logo, my car's make and model, and my name on it. First class!!!

It was 7:30 a.m. and we would be here until 4:00 p.m. Should be a long day, but it wasn't. It was a full day with 2 major happenings and a finale. The first happening was sitting with the car while spectators and the other car owners looked it over, asked questions, or just talked cars. The Marauder with its massiveness, gleaming black paint, and the 429 under the hood somehow stood out from the GTO and the AMX next to it. The spectators numbered in the thousands. I heard a quote of 30 thousand spectators from one of the staff. Needless to say it was a constant parade of people and conversation. Most of it was admiration and questions about the big Merc. The most popular questions/comments were: "I don't remember this car," "I've never seen one before," "It's huge," It's beautiful," and "they don't make them like this anymore." My most common answers were: "Yes it's rare," "It has a 6 body trunk," "It gets 30 miles to the tank full," plus a whole bunch of "Thank you's" for their kind words. There is a great pleasure in having someone appreciate your car and the time and effort you have put into it. It more than makes up for all the time and money spent restoring and caring for the car. Well, at least on this day it did for me.

The other happening that day was walking around the Concours grounds and looking at the cars. There is no way that I can convey this experience. The quality, uniqueness, history, etc. of the cars was unbelievable. *One-off* cars, and cars that were one of one, or two of three remaining, were commonplace.  The coachwork, luxuriance and the mechanics of the older cars were awesome. As I stated, I cannot describe the total scope of the Concours. There was just too much too see. I took pictures until the battery in my camera died.

That brings me to the finale. A few minutes before the awards were to begin the Concours staff went out to the winners of each class (3 in each) and had each of their cars line up for the presentation. One by one each class winner would drive his or her car up to the podium where the chairman and members of the Concours Committee would interview each owner while in their car. The interviews were over the loud speaker while pictures were being taken of the cars and their owners.

The interviews were interesting and provided additional information beyond what was on the display card for that car. Everything was professionally organized and executed without fault. *I thought this was the perfect end to the day.* Although having my car in that lineup might have been more perfect. *Who knows, maybe next year?* All in all it was a special weekend. Here's hoping the rest of my Bucket List goes as well.

I do have to say, that out of 150 cars in the Concours, *my Marauder was the only Mercury.* I did not expect that. There are a lot of outstanding Mercury's out there. I see them in car shows and Classic car magazines. I can only hope that in the future other Mercury owners will apply to Hilton Head for the inclusion of their car in the Concours d' Elegance. Believe me, it is a worthwhile event. While my Marauder wasn't judged, it was received very well by both the spectators and the other car owners. Based on the comments from spectators, Concours staff and other car owners I think it represented Mercury owners very well. I will be going back to Hilton Head next year, car or no car, and I hope this time to see some very nice Mercury's there.

Chapter 10
Boca Raton Concours d' Elegance
More fun… more bumps… and Bambi…

Two months removed from an exciting trip to the Hilton Head Concours d' Elegance, I am surfing the internet to check what car shows were upcoming in Florida and I see that there is a Concours d' Elegance event in Boca Raton on the 21st of February. I really enjoyed Hilton Head, mainly because it was an opportunity to show my Marauder X-100 someplace other than the West Coast of Florida where I have been showing it for the last 6 years. Hilton Head was fun-- mingling with new people most of whom had little or no knowledge of a Marauder X-100.

Part I: The Beginning

With Boca Raton being on the other coast of Florida, where I have never shown my car, I applied for entrance and it was accepted. I called Paulo, the driver that took my Marauder to Hilton Head. When I called him he said he was on the road and would check his schedule when he got back home. A few days later he called and said we were a go, so I made reservations at the Resort that was hosting the Concours. I did this because I was told I could walk to the Concours grounds from the resort. As I found out later the Concours grounds was the driving range for the resort's golf course.

My wife and I arrived the day before and Paulo was scheduled to bring the car in very early on the day of the Concours. Being somewhat anal, I wanted to arrive a day early to get the lay of the land, where the concourse grounds are in reference to the resort, where the transport could unload the car, how to get from the unloading point to the Concours grounds, etc. So off I went to scout the layout in an effort to ease my mind about the whole event. After an hour or so of convincing myself that no one on the resort's staff (We have a car show here?) knew anything about the Concours, I finally walked in the direction of the golf course and found someone putting up a sign for the Concours. He couldn't answer any of my questions, but he called Matt, who he assured me could answer my questions. When Matt arrived, in his golf cart, he gave me the grand tour and answered all of my questions.

After the tour ended, I could see only one possible problem. The road, actually a golf cart path, my Marauder would take to get to the Concours Grounds (Driving Range) was up a little hill along the side of the putting green. The path appeared to be barely wide enough for my Marauder and was banked at a 45 degree angle toward a deep ditch filled with trees. It was edged with some loose stuff that did not seem very firm for 4,300 lbs. of car. I had visions of my Marauder sliding down this 45 degree slope (well maybe only 30 degrees) into this ditch. Matt said it was not a problem, that all of the cars were going in that way. That didn't make me feel any better about it, but I thought I would wait until morning and watch a few cars go up the path and then make my decision (*To do what?*).

That night I couldn't sleep and kept thinking about my Marauder sliding down the bank into the ditch and massive trees scratching inch deep gouges into its side. Actually, the 2 lbs. or so of salami, pastrami, etc. that I ate as appetizers, followed by spicy meat, fish and chicken for dinner that night may have assisted in my not sleeping. In any case, when I rolled out of bed that morning I was pretty sure I was not taking my Marauder up the Boca Raton version of the Ho Chi Minh Trail to the Concours Grounds. *As I've said, I can be somewhat anal about my car. But that's why a 7 year old restoration looks like a new restoration.*

I got dressed and headed for the transport unloading area, passing the *sliding ski slope* of a cart path on the way. I met Paulo and told him not to unload the Marauder until I have a heart to heart with the Concours people. Determined to protect my Marauder from the *slippery slope*, I headed for the Concours check in area; when I turned a corner I almost got run over by Matt and his golf cart. As I began my spiel about the dangers of the *Thunder Road cart path*, Matt interrupted me and said "Okay, just go around to that paved road right there and come in that way--it's our backup entrance." Huh! Now you tell me? I was too relieved to be upset and immediately headed for the unloading area to get the Marauder.

After an easy ride through the *backup entrance* I checked in and then followed the golf cart, as directed, to the area reserved for Class 40, "American Collectables." It was a long ride as we passed gorgeous car after gorgeous car for what appeared to be miles. Class 40 was at the absolute end of the Concours Grounds/driving range. There were no yardage markers left on the driving range so I couldn't tell you what distance Class 40 was from the driving range tees. But I would bet my house that Tiger Woods couldn't drive a ball off those tees to within 300 yards of where Class 40 was parked.

Part II: The Concours

The distance was actually a good thing as it allowed for the 150 cars in the Concours to be spread out. Each class had its own area separated from the other classes (sometimes by a mound or a sand trap) and each car in its class had plenty of room. This gave the spectators, of which there many, room to leisurely walk around each of the cars without bumping into each other or the cars.

The quality and uniqueness of the cars was amazing. Although the obligatory Corvettes, Mustangs and Camaros were in evidence, and while not necessarily unique, their quality was outstanding. The pre-war cars, as always, stood out. The craftsmanship and style from those days, especially in the '30s can, in my mind, never be surpassed. The post-war cars were also impressive as the variety of these  cars at the Concours vividly pointed out the unique styling and character of the different makes and models through the '60s and early '70s. Of course the foreign cars were there; superb high quality cars that, among other things, highlighted the difference between European and American styling. The

Europeans were smaller and more stylish in a flowing sort of way. The old Jaguar XKE's would be a prime example of this styling. The Americans were larger and more *grandiose*. *Grandiose* I guess could be another word for luxury and chrome. The Cadillac's and Chryslers of the late '50s and early '60s were truly *grandiose*. Performance was another big difference. While the Americans believed cars were straight line rocket ships going from stop light to stop light, the Europeans believed that a car should be allowed to go around corners without tipping over.

Then there were the Exotics. The Ferraris, Lamborghinis, etc. are at home at stop lights and curves and considerably faster than the average Europeans and Americans. Of course you could buy a European car and an American car plus a few small islands in the South Pacific for the price of an Exotic. I don't believe I will ever own an Exotic, for a number of reasons, all of them being money. But I would be willing to pay a few dollars just to get the sound coming out of their exhaust pipes--to come out of the exhausts on my car. Just like a Harley Davidson motorcycle has a unique sound, the sound of a Ferrari at high rev is an unmistakable and eerily sensual song. *Hey! I can dream, can't I?*

Even with the distance, and all of the outstanding cars, the spectators and the other car owners all seemed to make the trip down to the end of the Concours to visit Class 40. The Marauder got a tremendous amount of love from spectators and car owners. It was easily as enjoyable as Hilton Head. *I guess I need to travel more.* Unfortunately the Judges also made the long trip to Class 40.

Judges and I don't seem to get along, at least not the ones in the major car shows. I think it's because I am a hard-headed stubborn person. Let me explain... I have a cluster of gauges on my steering column. They are not factory original. They are not dealer options. They are there because my car is not a trailer queen. I know, I had my car trailered to this Concours, like a trailer queen. But consider that the other option was to drive a 40 year old car 375 miles across the state of Florida, through the Everglades and its billions and billions of bugs. I would have had to leave a month early in order to have time to scrape the bugs off of the car, sand it down and repaint it. As it is not a trailer queen, I drive this 40 year old car to shows that can be 150 to 200 mile round trips on Interstates and back roads. I am not going to do it with just idiot lights. I need gauges to tell me when I am getting in trouble, not 40 year old idiot lights that tell me I am in trouble and it is too late to do anything about it. I could take these gauges off, only 10 to 15 minutes of effort, but I am stubborn. Most shows/judges allow you to have radial tires on your car, as long as they are period correct, because they are a safety factor. I believe my gauges are a safety factor, and they are period correct, and I feel they should be allowed with no penalty. But not today! So no trophy for me, but still some weird sense of satisfaction for a stubborn, troubled man...

Part III: The Magnetic Chair

I sometimes talk about my Marauder as a magnet for people. The big shiny black beast seems to draw in people like a magnet. Spectators and car owners bypass other cars and go straight to the Marauder. Cool!! As you know, when a magnet is in close proximity to another piece of metal, that piece of metal will take on some magnetic properties.

Well, that may have been what happened to my extra chair. I normally take a folding chair with me to car shows. Only one chair, as my wife is not into cars and only occasionally walks through the shows. On this trip I took 2 chairs as there was a slim possibility that she would come to the show should one of the following possible scenarios occur: (1) All of the stores within 200 miles would be closed. (2)She would take a wrong turn. (3) Hell would freeze over. So when I arrived I set up both chairs, initially using the second chair to house my reading material.

As I sat down, almost immediately, or magnetically, Paulo my transport driver shows up saying he parked the transport close to the show and walked over. So I offered him a seat in the *magnetic chair* that I normally don't have with me. Paulo and I bonded for a few hours and then he left to go visit his sister who lives in the area. I took this time to make a break for the restrooms, some 1,000 yards away, up by the driving range tee. When I returned my wife was sitting in the chair (the magnetic chair?). She said people had questions about the car and she didn't have the answers. She had stopped to visit because her friend, who she was going shopping with, was running late and wouldn't be around for about 2 hours. A pleasant two hours passed, with, I hope, my wife getting a better appreciation of my car and why I do this show thing. When my wife left I made another long trek to the restroom.

Where's the Restroom???

Throughout the day there had been a woman in another car class about 100 yards across and to the right from me that has been nothing but animated all day. She appeared to be dressed in something that was clingy and tight, and it looked very good on her, at least from this distance. As I returned from the restroom I notice that this animated clingy-dressed woman is talking to someone and pointing toward my car. I paid no attention and sat down. When I looked up again, the same woman was at a different car class and again pointing toward my car. I no sooner picked up my magazine again and started reading when I heard a voice. It was the clingy-dressed woman reeling by my car, saying she loved it, and heading for the chair. *The magnetic chair strikes again.*

With a bottle of Miller Lite waving in one hand she slumps down in my chair. She is slumped down so far her head is lying on the arm of the chair and she is looking up at me. She says, "Hi I'm Bambi" and starts talking. It is pretty clear that she has had more than enough to drink, but she is pleasant and likeable so no harm done. She bubbles on telling me about the cars she's owned and the cars she likes, especially my Marauder which she says she loves. Then she suddenly stops talking about cars and points to a well dressed woman over in the exotic car area and says sadly, "I told her that I thought she had a lovely frock on, and she told me I was naked." Huh! I had no idea what this meant, and I didn't ask, but over the next hour, sitting in my magnetic chair, she repeated the "She told me I was naked" story many times.

After more stories about the cars she liked, she then proudly told me the story of when she broke off the key to her car in the ignition. She said that she couldn't get that part of the key out at first but then she sucked it out... Pursing her lips and making a loud animated sucking sound she demonstrated this technique. Since, so far, I had been at a continual loss for words with her, I continued this tactic and said nothing. Then her boyfriend and another friend suddenly pulled up in a golf cart, both waving bottles of Miller Lite. Bambi introduced us and told them how much she loved the Marauder. The boyfriend asked her if she wanted her picture taken with the Marauder. She yelled yes and jumped up from the magnetic chair.

Well! It was then I realized what Bambi was talking about when she said the woman had said to her that *"she was naked."* Bambi's outfit was a clingy tight thing made up of a mesh like material, like you would have in a cardigan sweater, except that the mesh was very wide. As Bambi looked down at me and asked if it was okay to take the picture, also looking down at me were both of her nipples peering out through the holes in the mesh. Instantly she was up and dancing around the Marauder while her boyfriend took pictures. Her boyfriend then invited me to join Bambi and them at his yacht for an evening party. He said it was okay to bring my wife, as it was a wife friendly party. I said I would think about it.

They left in their golf cart and fearful of what the magnetic chair would bring next, I immediately put it back in the trunk of the Marauder. As the show ended and I was driving the 1,000 yards through the Concours/driving range to the exit, I all of a sudden heard someone yelling out, "*Ed!, Ed!, Ed!.*" I looked out the window and there was Bambi bouncing up and down and waving to me as I passed.

Accelerating slightly, I began to think that maybe it isn't the chair that is magnetic, maybe it's me!

Or maybe not…

Part 4 – The Wife Friendly Party.

Just kidding, we passed on the party…

Chapter 11
Welcome to White, Georgia
A tribute to the people, and the place, that saved my life...

Where The Heck Is White, Georgia

I've had a hell of a ride through this crazy, but fun, world of classic cars. And when I think back as to how this all started, my fondest memories go back to *where* it started. My re-birth from a discontented retiree to an active member in this loosely coupled, but tightly knit, world of classic cars started in the little North Georgia town of White. This town and the people in it kick-started my life and I thank them very much for that.   The following, I hope, spells out how I feel about my *re-birth* place: **White, Georgia**.

When my friend Roger Papp talked me into restoring a classic car and offered to help me do it, he said he had the tools and expertise to do most of it. What he couldn't do would not be a problem, as the expertise he didn't have was all around where he lived.

Welcome to White, GA, Roger's home town, a little community in the rolling mountains of North Georgia on a 2 lane road without even a stop light. A post office, a diner, and a car junk yard are the highlights of the center of town (if a town without a stop light can have a center). In most parts of the country, if you were driving through a *no-stop-light* small town like White, Georgia, and you blinked, you would miss the town entirely. If you were on GA State Road 411 passing through White and you blinked, you would miss about a dozen gorgeous classic cars. White is a suburb of Cartersville, Georgia (if a town of some 20,000 people could have a suburb). Calling White a suburb of Cartersville is a stretch, as White is some 8 miles from Cartersville, but if a *no-stop-light* town is not a suburb, then what is it? I'll tell you what it is. It is a population of people that seem to revolve around a world of classic cars. When I talk about classic cars I mean anything to do with old cars, classic original cars, street rods, custom cars, race cars, etc.

The junkyard in the center of town (*Old Car City*) is not a graveyard of junk cars but a repository for classic cars of all types, makes, and models. Some are restorable and for sale, while others are only usable for parts to feed the appetites of the local, and not so local, classic car restorers. The owner of *Old Car City* recently opened a sealed room in which he had stored a car which had once belonged to Elvis. There was quite a lot of news coverage about the big event, which consisted of breaking through a cinder block wall to get to the car.

Directly across the street from *Old Car City* is the diner I mentioned, *Wes-Man's Restaurant*, which has been around since forever. The first thing you notice when you near the diner is one or more classic cars parked outside. At the front edge of the parking lot is an old panel truck (1950s era) on which *Wes-Man's* owner paints the name of friends and family members for their birthday or special occasion. It is said that there are so many coats of paint on the panel truck that the paint is all that is holding the old truck together.

WesMan's Birthday Truck

A couple of years ago someone *"moved"* the truck and there was a reward put out for its return. The truck mysteriously appeared 2 days later across the street in the *Old Car City* lot. There is still a lot of speculation about who moved the truck and why. My question is: where could you possibly hide a truck in a town as small as White, GA? Maybe it was across the street all the while, but everyone was too busy restoring their classic cars to notice?

When you approach *Wes-Mans* you notice a number of plastic bags filled with water hanging just outside the diner and when you go inside the diner there

Bag of water...

are more hanging plastic bags of water. If you ask the waitress what the bags of water are for she will tell you they are thermometers. **Huh!** She explains that if the bag of water is hard then it's cold out and if the bag is soft then it's warm out. **Okay!** Also the bags, and the water in them, double as a fire protection system. **Okay! Okay!** After much laughter and banter back and forth she finally explains that the bags resemble a wasp's nest, at least to the Georgia population of house flies it does, and keeps the flies away. Does it work? I don't know, but there weren't any flies around. *Wes-Mans* is the lunch gathering spot for the working population of White and is a hotbed of conversations on classic cars and war stories of back-in-the-day moonshine runs. Recently, another friendly diner, *Dee's Road Kill Café* (an appetizing name), opened to handle the lunches of the increasing population of classic car owners in this small town.

Well, at least the post office is not a center of classic car activity. Right? Not so fast, if you enter the post office on any day of the week you will see packages from *Summit, JEG'S, Year One* and other auto parts companies stacked behind the counter waiting for some classic car guy to pick them up. If you're into classic cars then you will love White, Georgia. *Like I do!*

Why North Georgia?

Why is North Georgia so into old cars, hotrods and race cars? *I don't know!* The area's history of moonshine stills and fast cars making moonshine runs might be a factor, but whatever the reason if you look around you will most assuredly see that it truly is a hotbed of classic and hotrod cars. While White itself does not have a car show/ cruise-in, its neighbor Cartersville has a cruise-in every first Saturday during the warmer months that fills the center of town along the railroad tracks with all kinds of outstanding classics and customs. Live bands play and what looks to be the entire population of Carterville turns out. Some 25 miles to the west in Rome, Georgia, there is a monthly cruise-in that regularly exceeds 200 classic cars, rods and trucks. Another 25 miles to the northeast in Canton, Georgia, there is a monthly cruise-in that boasts 500 plus cars, rods, trucks and other forms of vehicles. It has been said that the Canton cruise-in is the largest on the east coast.

From Canton, another 25 miles to the east is Dawsonville, Georgia, home of NASCAR racer Bill Elliott ('Awesome Bill from Dawsonville') which has monthly shows and once a year has the *Moonshine Run Festival* celebrating the moonshine industry, which at one time was centered in this part of Georgia (some say it still is). It is not unusual for the *Moonshine Run's* Grand Marshall to be one of those legendary NASCAR names like *Johnson, Yarborough, or Allison*. Featured among the 500 plus cars at the festival, are the *high powered* 1940s and '50s cars that delivered the moonshine from the stills up in the mountains to the speakeasy's in the local towns. They were souped-up cars, with tanks full of moonshine, making high speed runs down winding two lane mountain roads, ever on the lookout for revenuers, to make their deliveries. With all of these fast cars and fast drivers, it was natural that in their spare time they would be racing each other. This is why Dawsonville is considered by many as the racing birth place for what eventually became NASCAR. I am sure in talking

about car shows and cruise-ins that I am missing a lot of North Georgia towns and a lot of car shows and cruise-ins, but if you are ever in North Georgia it would be hard not to find one.

Who's Who in White, Georgia?

Okay, let's get back to White, Georgia. On the side of one of the rolling mountains on the outskirts of White, on a winding road just a stone's throw from Allatoona Lake, is where Roger, and his neighbors live. This little area contains my *Who's Who* in White: people that have both helped and inspired me in my entry into and my ongoing travels/travails in the world of classic cars. These people are prime examples of White, Georgia's passion and excellence in classic cars.

The Wizard of White...

Well, not really a *Wizard*, but if you look at some of his finished works and compare it to what they looked like before

he started you might think he was a *Wizard*. Roger's neighbor Brad Cline owns and operates *Thunder Valley Customs*, a custom car fabrication shop in White. Brad has had some of his creations featured in many of the national car magazines like *Hot Rod* and his cars have won top awards in many national car shows like *Good Guy's*. In the movie *Field of Dreams* it was said, "If you build it they will come." In the case of *Thunder Valley Customs* it's, "If you come they will build it." It doesn't matter what it is, if you can conceive of it in your mind Brad can put it in your garage.

My experience with Brad began when Roger and I had my '69 Marauder finished to the point of it being ready for paint and a little body work. Roger said we should go see Brad to get it done. Brad has a top of the line shop and specializes in custom work and he loves the creativity involved in it. The idea of just doing some minor body work and painting my big Marauder black was not exactly Brad's thing. Roger was persuasive--Brad was his friend--Brad agreed to do it. I was ecstatic.

A month later, after 3 weeks of block sanding the sides of the Marauder, what came out of Brad's shop was the straightest, blackest, 19 foot long car I have ever seen. As car guys know, black paint shows up every flaw, dimple, etc. on a car. Get out your magnifying glasses and microscopes, you won't find a flaw, dimple, etc. on the car. *Absolute Magic!!!* When I picked up the car from Brad and thanked him for the outstanding job, he said, (kiddingly, I think) "Don't even think about bringing another one of these back to me." I guess 3 weeks of block sanding is not very exciting or creative, but it is definitely very professional.

The Wiseman of White...

We have all heard stories about the Northern city slicker that comes down South to out slick the Southern good ole boys, and finds himself totally out-slicked. I don't know how many of these stories are true but if one of them Northern city slickers (or anybody) came to White, Georgia, to out-slick

Roger's neighbor Bud Layton... *Never happen*!!! In his denim bib overalls and with his slow Southern drawl, you could

mistake him for the caricature of a good-ole-boy, a country bumpkin, etc. Nothing could be further from the truth. Bud is a shrewd businessman, an entrepreneur, a classic car guy and, yes, a good-ole-boy in the best sense of the word. Bud was my friend Roger's mentor for restoring classic cars, so in a way through Roger, he was my mentor also. Bud has been heavily involved with the *National AACA (Antique Automobile Club of America)*, and several regional car club chapters in North Georgia since their inception. He is a walking encyclopedia on classic cars, especially Fords.

Visiting Bud, if you're a car guy, is like visiting Disney World for the first time as a kid. There is *Parts Car World*, a field of classic cars (which Bud refers to as his pasture) whose only purpose in life is to provide used parts to the classic car restorers of the world. Next to it is *New Old Parts World*, multiple buildings filled with new parts for old cars. *New Old Parts World* came about because years ago when Bud was just beginning to restore cars, long before "*eBay*", he had to go shopping for these parts at any and all car dealerships he could find. Mostly the dealership would have its old parts back in some remote storage area and Bud would go through these boxes of parts looking for the part he needed. It didn't take Bud long to realize that he wasn't the only one going through this exercise of trying to find parts for classic cars. In a stroke of genius Bud decided to go to the Ford dealerships and offer to buy up all of their new old parts. Consequently if you need a part for your classic Ford, skip "eBay" and call Bud.

Next to *New Old Parts World* is *Restoration World*, workshops and storage for the restoration of Bud's latest acquisitions. On my last trip there I saw a rare Ford Talladega completely restored and only needing some minor brake work before it moves next door to *Museum World*. *Museum World* contains Bud's collection of cars and memorabilia. Beautiful cars and unique memorabilia that take you back to a time when cars had character and individuality, like the people that drove them. Like Bud...

Bud's Talladega

The best part of the museum is the *Tour Guide*. There is a story behind every car and every piece of memorabilia in the museum. The *Tour Guide* (Bud) knows these stories and is more than willing to talk about them. If you think stories about cars and memorabilia can be boring, then you have never spent any time with Bud. His past experiences as a pilot, race car driver, etc. and his passion for all things automotive bring to life the cars and memorabilia in Museum World.

Like *Disney World*, *Bud's World* keeps changing and getting better. Bud has built and is continuing to update, a 1950s Gulf service station, out of one of the car garages on his property. He has just about finished the exterior and is planning on finishing the interior to include a wood-burning stove in the *office area* and putting one or two of his old cars in the service stalls. All of the signage, gas pumps and service station stuff are *authentic*. There are no reproductions in *Bud's World*. Everything is real and authentic, like Bud.

The <u>Whippersnapper</u> of White...
When we think of someone as a whippersnapper, we

think of a young inexperienced kid, probably wet behind the ears. My old and dear friend Roger Papp is not a young kid but, in the years of White, Georgia, where resident families date back multiple generations, he is the *young* whippersnapper. Roger having been a resident of White for only the last 15 years is the proverbial *"new kid on the block."* Roger was always a *car guy* but moving next door to Brad and Bud he became a true classic car guy, restoring cars under Bud's tutelage and finishing them to perfection with Brad's wizardry. Roger is not just a neighbor of Bud and Brad but a friend that will do anything for them, and they likewise for him. It is an amazing and enviable relationship to a car guy like me.

If you visit Brad's shop, *Thunder Valley Customs*, and ask the staff about Roger, they'll say, besides being a friend, that Roger has no fear and will take anything apart, a valued trait for a classic car restorer. Also, jokingly, they will mention his *ability* to put things back together. Tales of drills gone wild, etc. highlight stories of Roger's early years as a car restorer. Roger became an expert car restorer under Bud and Brad's tutelage. A tribute to the quality of work that Roger does, and to the mentoring abilities of Bud and Brad, is the quality of the restoration of my Marauder X-100 that resulted in its being featured in a number of magazines and Concours d' Elegances'. Did I forget to mention the numerous national awards Roger's cars have reaped over the past years? With the restoration of classic cars comes the requirement to house these cars. So Roger, the perfectionist, with his own two hands, converted the basement of his house into a *Rolls Royce/Bentley* class showroom for his classic cars. Soon realizing that you can't restore and maintain classic cars in a *Rolls/Bentley* showroom,

Roger built a standalone 3 stall garage and extended storage facility for his restoration work and his growing family of classic cars. Not bad for a young whippersnapper and really great for my friend.

Wrapping up White, GA.

White, Georgia, is my favorite small town. Being a car guy I suppose it's understandable that I feel this way. But White, and its next door neighbor Cartersville, are more than just a hotbed of classic cars. White, with a post office but no stop light and Cartersville, with its brick buildings made from Georgia red clay and train tracks running through the center of town, are, to me, a modern version of the small town images that Norman Rockwell portrayed in his paintings. If you're ever in Atlanta, consider taking a ride about an hour northwest on I-75 to White, GA, have lunch at *Wes-Mans Diner*, tour *Old Car City*, have dinner among the brick buildings in Cartersville and most of all enjoy the southern hospitality of North Georgia. Oh yeah, if it's on a weekend, be sure to check out one of the local car shows/cruise-ins, and if you do be sure to say hello to Roger, Brad and Bud for me...

Epilogue...

Well, it's been a hell of a ride so far, and I am not finished yet. I am a classic car guy and I will continue to be one for as long as I can. I see new and bigger mistakes in my future, some fun and some maybe *not* so much fun.

As an example of *not* so much fun is the 1949 Mercury coupe in Chapter 8. It was, and still is, a project car. A *very expensive* project car! I had visions of James Dean when I bought it. It didn't end up being James Dean's really cool cruiser, and I didn't become James Dean. Instead; it is the reason my wife does not have her new kitchen, it is the reason our vacation to Hawaii is cancelled, it is the reason I am moonlighting as a Wal-Mart greeter, and mostly it is proof that there is hell-on-earth.

I wanted to write more than one chapter on the '49

Mercury in this book, but its story, along with the mistakes I made, is longer than this book.

So I continue my ride, bump after bump, through this Crazy World of Classic Cars. Now it's your turn. Go to your local car show, enjoy the music, enjoy the cars, talk to the car guys, and get hooked on classic cars. Try it you'll like it!

Oh Yeah! Be on the lookout for my new book coming soon. It's the story of my '49 Mercury. It's titled:
"I Can't Blame Roger for This One, Or Can I?"
"I am not, and never will be, James Dean…"

References: Pictures of the Widow, the Beast and the 49 are on my web site at:
http://community.webshots.com/user/edwardzed

Videos of the cars are available on **"youtube.com"**.
Search on **"edwardzed"**.

Addendum...

A Professional Author?

I became a writer by accident. I was forced to write an article to get my car into a magazine. After I wrote the article, I realized I liked writing and began writing articles for magazines. They were all freebies. I didn't get paid to write them. I didn't expect to. I was learning how to write. All of the articles were about my car or my experiences in the classic car hobby, and all were written in a satirical form. Writing about something I experienced, and making fun of it, was easy for me. It was just telling a story.

Well I decided to write a serious article about the 1969 Marauders. It would include the history of the Marauder, specifications, etc. Something I had never done before. When it was finished I tried to get it published in a national magazine and I was told by *ALL* the magazines that they had their own writers, so the answer was always "No thanks". It was very frustrating. Finally I tried some of the overseas magazines and an email came back from Classic American Magazine, a British magazine, saying that they would publish the article if I had quality pictures

I sent the pictures. They said they were great and asked for an address where they could send the check. **CHECK??? HUH???** I replied that I was just interested in getting the article (my first serious article) published, not getting paid for it. I was told that they (Classic American Magazine) paid for articles. *And I was paid*--A rather nice sum by the way -- *I must be a "Professional Author"???*

The article, titled "X Marks the Hot" had the byline: *"Words and photography: Ed Zukusky."* **Pretty cool!**

And they spelled my name right on the check…

This is an edited version of that article...

'X' Marks the Hot

According to Ford, the 1969 Mercury Marauder X-100 brought the Marauder name and performance back to the Mercury line-up after an absence of several years...

Marauder X-100

In 1969, Mercury reintroduced the Marauder nameplate into its line-up of full-sized cars. This new Marauder followed the same blueprint as the earlier Marauders, combining big-car luxury with muscle-car performance. The earlier Marauders, introduced in 1963, initially were fastback versions of Mercury's full-size line-up. While this resulted in a sleeker, more stylish-looking car for the buyer, this fastback version was in fact a direct result of Mercury's decision to become a major player in stock car racing. The aerodynamics of the fastback roofline was a necessity for Mercury to compete on the stock car racing circuit.

While these early Marauders were not initially defined as performance cars, the buyer readily could, and did, choose performance options, and fittingly Mercury's Marauder line of engines provided that. The Marauder 390 cu. in. engine was available in 250 hp and 300 hp along with a Super Marauder 330 hp version. Also available was the monster Super Marauder 427 with 410 or 425 hp versions built specifically for the race track. There were 500 of the 427s built the first year and all but a very few went to the racing community. These 427 Marauders made a name for themselves on the race track and the 390 Marauders made a name for themselves on the street. While Mercury discontinued the Marauder name after 1965, the reputation they built on the track and the street lived on.

In 1969, Lee Iacocca, fresh from his success at Ford with the Mustang, was given the Lincoln-Mercury Division as a reward, and he decided to bring back the Marauder as a completely new Mercury model built on a shortened Marquis wheelbase. Mercury felt that the older muscle-car buyer was ready for a luxury muscle car, not a stripped-down, big-engine intermediate car. At the top of this new model line would be the Marauder X-100.

The Marauder X-100 was the performance version of the new Marauder. It was powered by Ford's new 429 cu. in. big-block which put out 360 hp and produced a whopping 480 lbs. ft. of torque at 2,600 rpm. This big-block power was harnessed to Ford's rock-solid C6 automatic transmission and nine-inch rear. The 429 was a robust engine with 10.5:1 compression, aluminum pistons, forged rods and it drank only 99 octane leaded gas. Let's just say it wasn't your typical *family Mercury.*

The X-100 differed externally from the standard Marauder as it rode on H70 x 15 tires wrapped round Kelsey-Hayes aluminum wheels, with fender skirts adding to a lower sleeker look and X-100 badges on the front quarters. Inside the X-100 it had all the luxury you expected from Mercury, along with optional bucket seats, console and horseshoe floor shifter. Like the earlier Marauders, it was a full-size car, 4,300 pounds and 221 inches long riding on a 121-inch wheel base.

As you approach the X-100, you immediately notice its size. It's bigger than anything built today. But the lines are smooth, with a Coke-bottle shape highlighted by a discrete double pinstripe that runs the length of the car. The front end is pure Mercury Marquis with its hidden headlights and massive grille.

The back has a tunnel roofline unique to the Marauder. In 1969, Mercury painted the trunk and the area within this tunnel roofline with a *matte finish,* part of a two-tone paint scheme that was standard for the Marauder. Interestingly, almost 50 percent of the X-100 buyers elected the option '*two-tone delete"* to get a solid color car and also saving a sum of near $125.

Behind The Wheel
Slide into the Marauder's bucket seats and you immediately notice the luxury, but what impacts you the next is the sheer amount of room. Although the car is 76 inches wide, you'd swear it is 10 feet wide. The back seat is your living room couch, only bigger and more luxurious. Wood grain is everywhere. It is a real a class act.

But Mercury, true to its luxury heritage, did not put any gauges on the X-100, just indicator lights. This particular X-100 has sixties style aftermarket gauges and a tachometer on the steering column, and they look like they belong there.

Turning the key, the 429 starts immediately. The aftermarket mufflers give it a mellow tone. Gun the engine and you get that harsh sound that lets you know that hidden beneath all of this luxury is pure raw muscle. Put your hand on the horseshoe shifter and everything changes.

You've slammed pistol grips, round ball knobs, sticks, and so on before, but the horseshoe shift feels both natural and menacing at the same time. The aftermarket tach and gauges stare at you and the exhaust rumbles. The luxury car is gone. Sound and power take over. You're in a muscle car.

Acceleration comes quickly, leaving a wide streak of rubber on the road behind you. The 480 lbs. ft. of torque helps this 4,300 pound car come off the line faster than you could believe and soon all 360 horses are gulping air and 99-octane gas at an expensive rate. Back-in-the-day car magazines tested the X-100 in less than 16 seconds in the quarter mile, but you know this car can go faster, *you can feel it!* You have 4300 pounds of luxury around you that can cruise the highway with a top-speed of 124 mph and you're ignoring the highway and you're looking for a stoplight and some competition!

The 1969 Mercury Marauder X-100 is a beautiful, luxurious muscle car that has been mostly ignored. It was ignored when it was built--only 5,635 were sold and it has been ignored for all the years since then, and now very few remain, too many of them in need of restoration or beyond help. It has been called *"The last of the full-size muscle cars,"* and you're sitting in one and it's the only one you can remember ever seeing.

Maybe the only one you will ever see and, for now, you're cool with that.

Ask The Man Who Owns One...
My father raced four-banger Fords on dirt tracks when I was a kid, so owning fast cars was natural to me as I got older. I owned a 1963 Chevy 409, a '69 Charger R/T, a '68 Torino GT and a '70 Chrysler 300, and then marriage and a family came along. It was a long time between muscle cars until eight years ago when I bought the Marauder X-100. It had been sitting in a garage in Ohio for eight years, at the bottom of a list of cars to be restored. It was part of one of those *"got to sell this one, so I have money to restore that one"* scenarios.

As it turned out the, the car had about 50,000 miles on it and 47,000 of those miles were from 1969-1997 in Colorado and California. The drive train was original and had never been out of the car. A tune-up and changing fluids were all that was needed to make this my daily driver. The interior, engine compartment and trunk had accumulated eight-plus years of crud but a lot of elbow grease and detailing fixed that. The A/C didn't work, but replacing a valve ($150) took care of that. The problem area was the body. There was no rust (thank you, California), but the paint was showing its 35 years. Unbelievably, when the car was delivered to me and unloaded from the trailer, the driver scraped the side. So some minor body work and a paint job were in order.

The short version is that Roger Papp, who did most of the elbow grease and detailing on the car, convinced his neighbor Brad, who owned Thunder Valley Customs, a rod and custom shop in White, GA., with a resume of cars in *Hot Rod* and other magazines, to paint the car.
After six weeks waiting to get into the shop, followed by three weeks in the shop, what came out was not a daily driver. The

car was perfect, with the deepest black paint I had ever seen. I was literally afraid to take the car out on the road--it took a while to get over that. Now I try to put 40 to 50 miles a month on it, including some high-speed time on the interstate - the engine loves high RPMs. And yes, I do look for stoplights and competition - it may be 'show pretty,' but it's a muscle car and it needs to be driven like one. At least that's my story and I'm sticking to it. – *Ed Zukusky*

Addendum
Part II

This is a collection of fictional stuff I wrote while under the spell of classic cars. Each is an example of a warped mind trying to make sense of the world he was thrust into.

1. SELLING CLASSIC CARS.

After getting my Marauder featured in a national magazine, I was comfortable that I could sell it at a good price. While I sold the Beast on *eBay* (I was desperate), I wasn't sure if that was the right way to sell my Marauder. Roger's good friend Bud was a wheeler dealer in classic cars and a lot of this rubbed off on Roger, which got him into buying and selling cars. I discussed how to sell my Marauder with Roger, and he proceeded to inundate me with stories from his and Bud's experiences. I then began making trips with Roger to major swap meets in the South, watching Roger in action trying to sell and buy cars.

What I learned, over this time was that buying and selling classic cars was a sub-culture all its own in the Crazy World of Classic Cars. This is how my warped mind saw it.

Auctions...
One popular way to sell classic cars is to put them up

for auction and have people bid on them. There are many car auctions out there, and some of them are even on TV. I recently watched one on TV and it was hard to believe that it *really* was a car auction. First of all it was on TV, which makes it suspect at least. Secondly, I believe it's actually a reality game show. Take notice that all of the contestants are wearing funny costumes consisting of any combination of cowboy hats, Hawaiian shirts, beards and a trophy wife/girl friend. The show begins with the MC standing on a podium and begging the contestants, who are huddled together in an arena, to bid money for the cars. Meanwhile, there are people running around harassing the contestants with sharp edged clipboards and then screaming out bids for them. Why the contestants are not allowed to bid for themselves is beyond me and, I believe, violates every rule of game shows. As the bids continue, the MC gets really wound up and begins stuttering excitedly. The weird thing about the show is that there doesn't appear to be any winners, as no one ever gets a car. Each time the bidding on a car ends, the car is just taken away. Not having a winner upsets the MC, who is totally worn out from stuttering, and he angrily slams his hammer down on the podium. It's a pretty good show, but I bet if they replace the guy with the hammer and turn the show over to Judge Judy the ratings would go up. At least she would make *someone* pay for the cars--and she doesn't stutter a whole bunch.

    Then there are the cars: beautiful, rare and perfect cars; cars you can eat off the engine; cars you can comb your hair in the mirror finish of the paint; dazzling cars that make the perfect statue. **Yes, I say statue!!!** *Because you can't drive them,* as the mileage would go up and the price of the car would plummet, and because they might get dirty. They end up being statues, locked up in a garage so no one can see or touch them. Or they end up as statues in a museum where everyone can see then and again no one can touch them. **They're cars** *damn it! You're supposed to drive them!*

The clones are the fun ones. Clones are base models of classic cars that are modified to look like rare special models of that car. They look like the real thing, but they are just a fake. Everyone knows they are fakes, yet Classic Car Guys go into a bidding frenzy to buy one of these fakes. They spend 20 times what the car cost new, **TO BUY A FAKE!!!**

Everyone has their favorite cars. Among mine are the Hemi Cudas. I don't know much about who was responsible for these cars at Chrysler except for the obvious fact that they must have been color blind. Painting cars in different shades of vomit can't be something you do on purpose. I also like Carroll Shelby's cars. I last saw Carroll some five years ago, and while he was getting up there in years then, you couldn't miss that right arm with those bulging muscles. I suppose if you spent your entire life signing your name on cars you'd have muscles like that too.

I took my car to one of these auctions. (Not one of the TV ones, as I don't own a cowboy hat or a Hawaiian shirt). Before putting my car up for auction I wanted to get an idea as to how much I could get for it. So I called the auction and they said *"come on down"* **(are you sure this isn't a game show?)** and we'll take a look at it. So I clean and polish the car and go down to the auction to meet with Harvey, one of the brothers that run the auction. Well, Harvey looks the car over for about 30 seconds and asks, "What kind of car is it"? **Huh?** I tell Harvey it's a Marauder X-100. Harvey walks around the car again (for about a minute); you can hear the wheels turning in Harvey's head.

He stops and looks at me and says, "Who makes it?" **Huh?** I tell Harvey that it is made by Mercury. Again, the wheels start turning, and Harvey walks around the car again. Finally he stops walking, turns toward me, and *leans back against my car* with his butt and the palms of both hands--*on my recently waxed perfect paint job*. I violently unlock my trunk looking for my tire iron.

Harvey says, "We can get $75,000 for it."

I'm dumfounded. I close the trunk (actually I leave it somewhat open just in case I need the tire iron) and I ask Harvey, "Why do you think you can get that much?"

There go the wheels in Harvey's head again... "Because it's a Mercury er. er. er.--what did you say it was again?"

"It's a Marauder X-100."

"Oh Yeah, we get $75,000 for them all the time. Now, if you'll sign this paper and give me $1,000 in unmarked bills, you're in the auction." As I reach for the tire iron, **Logic** screams down to me... *Ah the hell with it, I'm outta here!!*

While *Rich Classic Car Guy* sells and buys perfect cars (statues) at auctions like Barrett Jackson, the guy on the street buys and sells, less than perfect cars at eBay Auctions. eBay is an online auction, so you never get to see the car that is for sale. Instead, there are pictures of the car (normally taken before the accident) and a write up by the owner documenting the level of perfection his car has attained. One of the best parts about eBay is that potential bidders are allowed to ask questions of the car's owner. The questions alone are worth the price of admission. These questions vary widely from something technical like; *"What is the coldest temperature the car's A/C can attain if the weather outside is 98 degrees with 85% humidity and the wind is from the south at 97 miles per hour with a heavy cloud cover"*; to something passionate like *"Is it a nice car?"* The owner's answer to both of the above questions was the same. *"Hell yea!!"*

Ads and Car Corrals...

Another way to sell a classic car is at the Car Corral. A Car Corral is an area in a car show where cars that are for sale must go. Cars with "For Sale" signs on them are not allowed in the car show itself. Apparently there is a stigma on cars that are for sale, or possibly an air borne disease that requires their separation from the perfection of the car show. Consequently they are regulated to the nearest cow pasture in an adjoining zip code. The Car Corral is sort of like a leper colony, ignored by the car owners in the show and, for the most part, by the spectators. So the car owners in the Car corral are busy trying to sell or trade their cars with each other. This would make a great Reality TV Show. I've often wondered why it was called a car "corral" until I realized that 97% of the cars in the car corral are Mustangs. *Ouch! That was bad!!*

The other way to sell cars is to advertise in newspapers, magazines, or on the Internet. These are my favorites. The ads are priced based on the number of words and pictures in the ad. *Cheap Classic Car Guy* goes with the basic ad, a minimum number of words and no pictures. It might read something like this:

For Sale: 55 Ford, $9,000 Call Leroy 888-555-1234.

Such detail!!! I don't know about you, but that sounds like the perfect car for me, it's everything I would ever want in a car... Duh! I know it's hard to believe, but that ad did not work for Leroy. So after 6 months Leroy upgrades the ad to:

For Sale: 55 Ford, $9,000 **Runs**, Call Leroy 888-555-1234.

Yea, I thought this one would do it too, but it just wasn't meant to be!!! So Leroy, tears in his eyes, second mortgage on his house in his pocket, signs up and pays for a picture upgrade. Luckily there is no need to take a new picture, as Leroy just happens to have an old Polaroid of the car. So the new ad is:

For Sale: 55 Ford, $9,000 **Runs Good** Call Leroy 888-555-1234.

And the picture is a grainy cracked overexposed picture of a black (I think) Ford with 4 inches of snow on the roof and hood of the car. Its parked on a recently rock salted driveway, *can you say "rust?"*, alongside Leroy's barbecue, which also has 4 inches of snow on it, with Leroy's house trailer making a perfect background setting. *A Saturday Evening Post cover picture, if ever there was one.* Of course, Leroy's car sold. It had to be the picture that did it. **Duh!!**

Then there are the Car Dealers. Their ads are loaded with beautiful pictures and detailed specification and comforting words of wisdom as to why you should buy this car. However, there are no prices in the ads, just a telephone number to call. *Uh Oh!! Grab on to something and hold on tight…* There is a reason why there is no price. The car dealer does not want to sell the car at a specific price. He wants to sell it to <u>you</u> at the highest price <u>YOU</u> will pay. So to protect yourself, if you call one of these dealers, the first thing you must do is say in a calm reserved voice, "How much is the car?" During the next 10 minutes you will hear everything you want to know about the car except the price. You need to keep repeating, "How much is the car?" during this period. If you are on the phone for more than 10 minutes without getting the price, the dealer wins. The Classic Car Dealer's special phone accessory computer *(they all have them)* that takes about 10 minutes to calculate and record your blood pressure, body temperature and most recent bank statement. Once it has this, it takes into consideration the time of day, the day of the month and then calculates the price of the car, **TO YOU!!!** Any comments you make about the car such as "Nice car," "I like the color," etc. become multiplication factors in calculating the price of the car, **TO YOU!!**

CASH BUSINESS…

A most important thing about selling classic cars is that it is a "Cash Business." No checks, no credit cards; it's strictly cash. Why you ask??? It's because the buying and selling of classic cars is a nontaxable tradition in the good ole USA. Uncle Sam knows this and merely winks and turns his head as mountains of cold hard cash change hands as classic cars are bought and sold tax free. It's easy to tell the difference between buyers and sellers at a classic car meet. The sellers are the ones with their pant pockets turned inside out kneeling beside their cars. The buyers are the ones with pockets bulging with $100 bills, carrying a bulging bag with more $100 bills and a Snidely Whiplash grin. While this would appear to be a mismatch, the end result of any match between them is always in doubt. It is a back and forth affair that goes something like this.

The buyer walks up to a gorgeous Hemi Cuda:

Buyer: Nice car what do you want for it?
Seller: I'm asking $100,000.

Buyer: Will you take less?
Seller: Well, maybe I'll take $75,000.

Buyer: How about $100? (As he slowly waves a hundred dollar bill in the sellers face.)
Seller: It's an original car with only 650 miles.

Buyer: OK, OK, I'll go $30,000.
Seller: It has a special one-of-one prototype Hemi engine built by the factory.

Buyer: OK, OK, OK, $50,000, take it or leave it.
Seller: That's not a fair price for this car, but I need the money; it's a deal.

They get in the car and the buyer counts out $50,000 in cash, which the seller recounts and pockets. The seller then rummages through the glove compartment and finds and signs the title over to the buyer. As the seller walks away, the buyer is ecstatically happy and has a big grin on his face as he admires the Hemi Cuda, which he always wanted and which he purchased at an unbelievable low price. The seller, as he walks away, also has a big grin on his face as he wonders who owned that Hemi Cuda he just sold.

2. Manufacturing Fun...

Classic Car Guy believes that the Auto Manufacturers are gods and he worships this deity and the exquisite automobiles that they built. But, let the truth be known...

Not all was perfect back-in-the-day...

Chrysler/MOPAR built some of the most rust prone cars ever conceived. This is why few exist today. It is rumored that many of the 69-70 Dodge Chargers rusted out while still on the showroom floor. It is also widely believed that the last station on the Chrysler assembly line was referred to in the factory as the "Bondo Station."

What Chrysler didn't realize, but Chevy did, was that rust normally formed where two or more body parts came together, allowing moisture to be trapped in this area. Thanks to Chevy's design engineers there are millions of old Chevy's left today because virtually none of Chevy's body parts ever touched or lined up correctly. Chrysler called it shoddy workmanship. Chevy called it "Creatively Randomized Automotive Panels" (CRAP)

Did you ever notice that when you went to a Chevy Dealer they only had 1 Corvette in stock and it was in the back of the air conditioned showroom away from the window? That's because some of the plastic *(fiberglass? Yea right!)* body parts had a tendency to melt whenever the sun was out or the temperature got over 70 degrees. Many have wondered where **"The Vision"** that became the Corvette Mako Shark concept car came from. It is believed that a Corvette driven by Zora Duntov was left outside over a hot weekend and melted. Upon seeing this, Zora, wielding a metal spatula like the masked Zorro would a sword, quickly redesigned the front bumper on this melted beauty and this *smooth flowing* design became the Corvette Mako Shark concept car.

Ford has for many years been known by the acronym

FORD (Fix Or Repair Daily). History supports this acronym. As an example, the 49 – 53 Ford flathead engines were great running engines. However, every external component that was required to make this great engine run was made by a company called Autolite, better known as <u>Ah-no-light</u>. The company was formed by 4 engineers that helped design the war machine that was Italy during World War II. These engineers, when sober, were masters of the art of "planned obsolescence," building quality products that have a fixed life time. Unfortunately, miscommunication between Ford (using the decimal system) and Autolite's Italian engineers (using Roman numerals) resulted in this fixed life time being days instead of years.

Ford's engineers created their own share of this Fix Or Repair Daily reputation, as they developed a silky smooth 3 speed manual transmission to transfer the horse power of these flathead engines to the rear wheels of the cars. These manual transmissions performed effortlessly and flawlessly *unless you decided to actually shift into another gear*. Shifting the 3 speed transmission quickly (hard), many times resulted in internal Shearing and Shrapnel-ing, quickly converting the 3 speed into a 1 speed (neutral) transmission. Ford engineers had a built-in safety feature should Shearing and Shrapnel-ing occur. The cars driveshaft would immediately disconnect (snap off) from the transmission and dig into the road stopping the car safely. This phenomenon known as All Hard Shifting Hurts Internal Things (AHSHIT) caused the creation of the first automotive aftermarket industry, a machine shop that manufactured aftermarket Ford gears actually made out of metal.

Yet, with all its problems, Ford can still proudly state that eight out of ten Fords are still on the road today. The other two eventually making it home.

Meanwhile, back at Chrysler, a corporate decision was made to go full bore into the muscle car market. Chrysler quickly started stuffing its powerful Hemi engine into every one of its car lines. The idea being that between NASCAR, Drag Racing and some of the idiots buying these cars, most of the cars would crash and burn before they had a chance (6 months to a year) to rust out and give Chrysler a bad name. *It worked!!!   How many original Hemi cars do you see today????*

Meanwhile Nash (No Automobile Styling Here) and Hudson (Huge Ugly Design, Styled On Nothing) went out of business. They bit the dust because, "America was not ready for the future of automobile styling." **Huh!!!** *No one ever said that, but you can bet that one or more of the TWITS that ran those companies thought that.*

With Nash and Hudson on the way out, Studebaker leaped forward and came out with their Hawk series of cars. The 57 Golden Hawk was the high point of Studebaker styling. This was followed, unfortunately, by the Obese Hawk, the Fat Ugly Hawk and the Non-Descript Hawk. This series of Hawks coincided with Studebaker's hiring of the Nash and Hudson design teams. As Studebaker began to fade away, the Nash and Hudson design teams began to eye American Motors.

American Motors continued to survive with its sporty AMXs and Javelins leading the way for this forward looking car company. Then, without warning, the Nash and Hudson design teams infiltrated American Motors.   Soon after, Gremlins attacked the company, wiping out the AMXs and Javelins. Following the Gremlin, the Pacer, a glass bubble with a lawnmower engine, appeared. This was followed by the Eagle, a 4 wheel drive car that looked like a nerd with his pants pulled up to his chest. Again, "America was not ready for the future of automotive styling." *This time I think someone actually may have said this.* <u>*Might have been Rodney Dangerfield*</u>*...*

Meanwhile, the Nash and Hudson design teams, riding

this wave of successes, then began to eye the Big Three (GM, Ford & Chrysler). In the only known cooperation between the Big Three companies, a general fund was created which guaranteed a life time income to the Nash and Hudson design teams on the condition that they never work in automotive design again. Unfortunately for the Big Three, the Nash and Hudson design teams were all Catholics and, as such, very prolific breeders. Years later, in the late '70s and early '80s, the numerous offspring of the Nash and Hudson design teams infiltrated the Big Three. *And the rest is history..*

3. SPAM

Back in Chapter 1 there is a reference to SPAM and peanut butter. This happens to be a true addiction with me. I know it's not good for the heart, but, for me, it's good for the soul. The recipe below pretty much documents how my relationship with SPAM started. By the way, the recipe below hangs in the SPAM Museum in Austin, Minnesota. YES!! There really is a SPAM Museum. *"http://www.spam.com/museum/"*. And YES!! The recipe is in it…

Title: SPAM & Peanut Butter Sandwich.
Description: SPAM and PEANUT BUTTER.

In 1962 I was in the US Army and stationed in Karlsruhe, Germany. I had been in Germany for a year and a half and had some leave time saved up. Three of us decided we would like to see what we could of Europe as long as we were here. While we had leave time saved, money was a different story.

We finally convinced one of our buddies, in a worse financial condition than us, that we would make his next car payment for him in exchange for using his car for our 30 day leave to see Europe. Being desperate, he agreed. We "borrowed" a US Army hex tent, blankets, gas stove, etc. Stuffed everything into our buddies Volkswagen Beetle and headed to the mess hall for supplies. The Mess Sergeant, a kindly soul, informed us that rations were for personnel while on post. As we did not have the money necessary to eat out every day during our trip, we were forced into plan B. We were able to locate some of our buddies who were on KP at the time. After much discussion, the best they could do to help us was to "find" a case of crunchy peanut butter and a case of Spam in the back of the mess hall, which we stuffed into the Beetle.

Off we went to tour Europe. Germany, Switzerland, Italy, Spain and France over the next 30 days! Camping out, breakfast was mainly coffee but lunch was the treat. As we drove, without plan or timetable, when lunchtime came we would stop in whatever town we were in and buy a loaf of the local bread and a bottle of the local wine. We would then sit alongside the road or in the local town park and eat cold Spam and crunchy peanut butter sandwiches washed down with the local wine. Life was good. The last Spam and peanut butter sandwiches of our trip were eaten on Easter Sunday in a small park across the street from Notre Dame Cathedral in Paris while watching people go to Easter Mass.

Since that time, much to the chagrin of my wife and son, I have continued my love affair with Spam to include Spam and peanut butter, Spam and American cheese (hot), Spam Chili, etc., etc.

Ingredients:

A Taste of Paradise...

For those of you who haven't tried Spam and peanut butter, it must be crunchy peanut butter and the Spam and peanut butter should both be cold from the refrigerator or hot from sitting in a car for days.. Fresh bakery bread is a plus. Good stuff. Add some wine and you won't remember it's SPAM... Enjoy

Directions: Lose inhibitions and dig in. **Number Of Servings:** Whatever you can handle.. **Preparation Time:** Depends on how much wine you have had.

4. BACK-IN-THE-DAY...

Did you ever think about the cars you owned back-in-the-day? Of course you have, we all have.

Well, it's a Friday and it's raining. It's also supposed to rain Saturday and Sunday. So, no car shows for me this weekend. Bored, I crank up my TIVO and start watching the American Muscle Car TV shows I had recorded. Somehow I can't bring myself to delete these shows after I watch them, so there are 22 of them on my TIVO waiting for me to watch them again and again. I randomly pick a show and start it up. Half way through the show, *I see my car*, a black 1963 Impala Super Sport 409. Not really *my actual car*, but close enough to cause me to flash back to the cars I used to own back-in-the-day.

I was born and raised in Scranton, Pennsylvania. My first car was a 1949 Ford 4-door flathead V8. It was our well-used family car that was handed down to me when I was 16. My Dad was a coal miner and a backyard mechanic that had raced cars on dirt short tracks, so he helped me make the 49 a bit faster than stock. I rewarded him by blowing out transmissions on an average of once a month. Actually, after I blew the *third* transmission, a not so subtle warning told me that this would be the last transmission I would blow.

By this time my "speed shift" into second gear was famous throughout the neighborhood. Kids would marvel at the bent shift lever and the missing ball from the end of the lever that had disintegrated during one of my famous speed shifts. Kids would borrow their father's car and come looking for me. And away we would go, down to a little two lane road behind the burning *Culm* dumps. (*Culm dumps were "mountains" of refuse from the mining of anthracite coal. Some of these "mountains" would catch fire and burn -- many burned for decades.*) This was our drag strip. At night the burning dumps lit up the area with vibrant multi-colored flames running up their massive sides, creating a surreal atmosphere that still lives in my memory. Drag racing, partying, parking, all in the glow of burning *Culm* dumps, was a part of my teenage years.

Back to the '49! The '49 was the common Ford dark blue color of that era. I painted it a light blue. Actually, my Father and I painted it. I mean my *Father* painted it. In any case it was light blue. My after school job, in my uncle's Walt's store, provided the money for light blue seat covers. I also bought some white vinyl material and covered the door panels and package tray. I came across a pair of '57 Mercury Turnpike Cruiser skirts that a kid down the block had. He said he found them on the side of the road. I traded him a 2 carb. "Y" manifold (I had somehow acquired) for the skirts. The light blue '49 with its Turnpike Cruiser skirts and bent shift lever was quite a sight as it rolled on through the neighborhood with its glass pack mufflers blaring. *Life was good, back-in-the-day*

I don't have any pictures of the '49, except in my memory. The Turnpike Cruiser skirts out-lived the '49 and ended up on my next two cars, a '50 Ford and '54 Ford. I sold the '49 to a neighborhood kid for $90. He paid me $40 up front. I never saw the rest of the money. Hey, that was my neighborhood, and that's how it was…**Back-in-the-day.**

'50 Ford with Turnpike Cruiser skirts